The Nonbroadcast Television Writer's Handbook

by William Van Nostran

Knowledge Industry Publications, Inc.
White Plains, NY

Video Bookshelf
The Nonbroadcast Television Writer's Handbook

Library of Congress Cataloging in Publication Data

Van Nostran, William.
    The nonbroadcast television writer's handbook.

    (Video bookshelf)
    Bibliography: p.
    Includes index.
    1. Television authorship.   I. Title.   II. Series.
PN1992.7.V36   1983   808'.066791   83-89
ISBN 0-914236-82-2

Printed in the United States of America

10   9   8   7   6   5   4   3   2   1

Table of Contents

List of Figures iv
List of Illustrations v
Introduction vii

1   The Writer in Nonbroadcast Television 1
2   How Television Works 9
3   Research Techniques: Getting to the Sources 19
4   Translating Research into Action: The Audience,
    the Objectives and the Content Outline 33
5   Visualizing the Program: The Treatment 47
6   Structuring the Script 65
7   Writing for the Eye 85
8   Writing for the Ear 101
9   Writing Unscripted Formats 119
10 Writing the Nonbroadcast Drama 141
11 Writing for Interactive Video 183
12 Careers in Nonbroadcast Television: Three Interviews 199

Appendix A: The Business of Nonbroadcast Scriptwriting 219
Appendix B: Professional Organizations 221
Glossary 223
Bibliography 227
Index 229

List of Figures

Figure 2.1 A Depiction of How Television Images are Created...... 14

Figure 3.1 Sample Research Agenda: Interviews 26
Figure 3.2 Sample Research Agenda: Observations 28

Figure 4.1 Audience Involvement and Ease of Measuring Results
for the Three Types of Objectives 39
Figure 4.2 Sample Content Outline 44

Figure 5.1 Examples of Mixed Script Formats 54

Figure 6.1 Camera Shots 66
Figure 6.2 A Custom Transitional Device 74
Figure 6.3 Advertising Agencies Generally Storyboard 81
Figure 6.4 An Illustration of Production Storyboarding 82

Figure 7.1 The Writer's Description of Settings and Backdrops 88
Figure 7.2 Painted Backdrops 90

Figure 8.1 Sample Script with Comments and Revision 110

Figure 9.1 Content Outline for an Unscripted Program 128
Figure 9.2 Interview Sheet for an Unscripted Format 132
Figure 9.3 File Card of Interview Comments
for an Unscripted Format 135
Figure 9.4 Edit Log Sheet for an Unscripted Format 136

Figure 11.1 Structure of Early Interactive Programs 185
Figure 11.2 Optical Video Disc Features That Aid
Instructional Design 189
Figure 11.3 At a Modern Interactive Study Carrel 190
Figure 11.4 The Branching of an Interactive Program 197

List of Illustrations

A nonbroadcast network can bring messages 5

The research stage... 25

Scenes from "Why Not Craig Cunningham?" 57

Showing scenes from real life 123

Interview subjects find it easier to talk in their work surroundings ... 125

Fictional characters give the writer flexibility 143

These four scenes from "Sexual Harrassment: Fact or Fiction" 158

*   *   *   *   *   *   *

ACKNOWLEDGMENTS

Writing a book is a lot different from writing scripts. For one thing, it takes a lot more endurance. In this case, Ellen Lazer, senior editor, and Ellen Smith, assistant editor, at Knowledge Industry Publications, Inc. have persevered through the sometimes protracted process of getting this book done.

The collaborative nature of creating material for the TV screen is a theme you'll find throughout this book. Over the years, my writing has been influenced through associations with many different directors and producers in the nonbroadcast field. One director in particular, James G. Libby, has not only been a close collaborator on TV projects, "devil's advocate" and business associate but also read drafts of this book in various stages and offered valuable suggestions. Finally, my appreciation to Ev Granger for photographic assistance and to the writers who took time for the interviews that appear in Chapter 12—Uli Monaco, Lois Gaeta and Casey Stone.

To Lynne, Kirsten and Kendra.

Introduction

This book had its genesis in workshops and seminars I've conducted on writing nonbroadcast television scripts. Most people attending such workshops did not hold full-time scriptwriting jobs, and their television writing experience was limited. There were always several people with print backgrounds seeking insight into the growing use of video cassettes for organizational communication. There were those in attendance who were trainers or instructional designers first—media writers second. Some participants came with solid television production credentials (including the producer-director-writer hyphenate breed). And always one could expect to find students with hopes of entering the field professionally. Those making their sole income as nonbroadcast TV writers were invariably in the minority.

Furthermore, workshops were attended by individuals representing tremendously diverse and varied organizations: Fortune 500 companies, independent production companies, hospitals, health care agencies, government agencies from the Department of Defense to municipal police and fire departments, colleges and universities—you name it.

Yet these people with such diverse backgrounds shared one thing in common: all sought ways of putting the medium of television to work for their organizations. They all seemed motivated by the need to answer the same basic questions: "How can I develop more creative programming?" "How can I present these dull subjects in an interesting manner?" "How can I make this abstract material more visual?"

In short, these people were bound together by the realization that the challenges facing the nonbroadcast television writer are totally different from those facing broadcast TV writers. In the Bibliography at the end of this book, you'll find that books on broadcast TV writing and motion picture screenwriting abound. But there are precious few books dealing with the special challenges facing the nonbroadcast writer. That's what gave impetus to this project. So I must acknowledge the contribution of those workshop participants through our joint explorations into the subject matter.

This book approaches the creation of video script as a process that takes the writer through a series of steps designed to yield a shooting script that is production oriented and appropriate for the project at hand. Although subject matter and video applications vary tremendously in the non-broadcast TV field, this process can be applied successfully to any project. The first phase begins with research and inquiry into the function of the video communication and leads to setting objectives based on a clear understanding of content and the dynamics of the viewing situation. The second and most critical phase involves developing a program concept, a creative strategy expressed through the television treatment. The third phase is the actual writing of a shooting script, cast in the language of television production terminology.

The book is organized to track with this process. After introductory material, Chapters 3 and 4 deal with the research and objective-setting phase. Chapter 5 suggests an approach to the conceptual phase, and Chapters 6, 7 and 8 treat the mechanics of writing the shooting script. Chapters 9, 10 and 11 offer more advanced material on specific program formats that the nonbroadcast writer often encounters. I've also included three interviews with writers working in the field to convey a sense of their milieu and daily activities.

I hope the book is useful to all those seeking to improve writing skills in this maturing arena of television communications. Beginning writers or those with a print orientation will find a process they can adapt to develop programming that is suitable for television and works for their organization and applications. More experienced media writers, familiar with the "nuts and bolts" material, should find that chapters on specific formats offer useful solutions to advanced writing problems.

1

The Writer in Nonbroadcast Television

THE NONBROADCAST TELEVISION MARKET

The goal of most broadcast writers is to reach the largest audience possible. Scripts with the mass appeal to garner big Nielsen numbers have the best chances of being produced and aired. But try asking any writer struggling with a nonbroadcast script who the audience is. Likely responses might be:

- The target audience is our field sales force. I'm writing a video presentation to introduce a new product, demonstrate the market potential and show the advertising and promotional materials.

- My audience is the orthopedic surgeon. This script describes new surgical procedures for treating fractures that also damage joint tissue.

- The script is a self-paced interactive program on the principles of centrifugal gas compressor design. The audience is the sophomore engineering student.

These responses say a lot about the nonbroadcast television market. As they suggest, the major areas are business, medicine and education. Government is a fourth market. Yet it is a diverse and fragmented market. Terms such as industrial television, private television, corporate television, professional television and narrowcasting have all been coined to describe this special market. No one is completely descriptive, though each defines a part. To clarify, here are some fairly universal attributes of the nonbroadcast television market:

- Nonbroadcast television programming is aimed at audiences who share a special interest in the subject matter.

- Content is targeted specifically to the audience's special interest.

- Distribution is normally accomplished by video cassette or video disc as opposed to a cable or broadcast transmission.

- Playback is usually under the direct control of the viewer.

- By placing video cassette or disc playback equipment in geographically dispersed locations, private television communication networks can be established.

THE AUDIENCE: READERS AND VIEWERS

So, what function does the writer perform in this specialized television field? Let's return to the question posed at the outset: "Who is the audience?" The hypothetical responses focused on descriptions of specialized, homogeneous viewing audiences: a field sales force; orthopedic surgeons; sophomore engineering students. This viewing audience, however, never reads the script. Finished television programs, after all, render scripts obsolete. Only a handful of people actually *read* television scripts. Yet their reaction to the content is as important as that of the viewing audience.

The Client/Content Experts

First, there is the client, who commissions the nonbroadcast television program and pays the bills. Because he funds the production, the client has a vested interest in the effectiveness of the completed program with the viewing audience. Unlike broadcast television, those who commission nonbroadcast television programs usually have no understanding of television production techniques. It's also rare to find a nonbroadcast client capable of visualizing the viewing experience from words on paper in script format. As a reader of television scripts, then, the nonbroadcast client and any designated content experts focus on content and tend to be sticklers for technical accuracy.

The Production Team

The second category of television script reader is the production team. As in broadcast television, the team is headed by a producer and a director (sometimes one and the same). In most cases, the scriptwriter works most closely with the director, so let's explore that relationship.

In contrast to the client, the director focuses singlemindedly on the fact that this script must be turned into a television program. The director wants to know how words on paper are supposed to become sights and sounds on video tape. Whereas the client or content expert nitpicks the technical content, the director's questions seek to understand what action the writer envisions on the screen.

- What kind of location footage do you see here?
- Do you see a male or female narrator? Why?
- Do you see stock footage helping to visualize these points?

Directors use the verb "to see" inordinately in conversation. The director, after all, gets to take the writer's words on paper and translate them into a viewing experience.

The Viewing Audience

In the final analysis, the scriptwriter, the client and the director all share responsibility for the final communication to a specialized viewing audience that must be defined. In the corporate environment, for instance, television presentations may be targeted to all employees in a company or organization. Frequently, however, the audience will be even more narrowly focused. Corporate video communications may be prepared for specific segments of the employee population: production workers, sales reps, clerical workers, supervisors and managers, even customers. In the health care segment of the nonbroadcast field, audiences may be neurosurgeons, third-year medical students, heart attack patients, expectant mothers. In education and training, subject matter and curriculum often dictate the audience: high school English students, senior biology students, vocational computer science students, operators of the 221 Word Processor.

Narrowcasting aptly describes the essence of communications aimed at a homogeneous, well-defined target audience. As the term implies, nonbroadcast television tends more toward the specific than the general. Look at this list of program titles:

"Meclomen: A Unique Compound"
"Update on Hyperlipidemias"
"The Perfect Serious $ Solution"
"Cash & Accounts"[1]

Not the stuff of which Hollywood blockbusters are made, yet these titles address specific products, services and medical, corporate or instructional subjects. "Meclomen: A Unique Compound" provides information for pharmaceutical sales representatives. The catchy "Update on Hyperlipidemias" is continuing medical education for physicians. "The Perfect Serious $ Solution" helps a large brokerage firm work with prospects for a tax-deferred annuity investment product. The business-like "Cash & Accounts" is actually a modern-day fantasy in which a contemporary genie helps an insurance company account analyst learn to use a new interactive computer terminal.

It stands to reason that when addressing such narrow audiences on these highly specific subjects, the writer should learn as much as possible about the characteristics of the group. Chapter 3 discusses the importance of knowing the audience and answering such questions as whether they will be receptive or resistant to the message and whether the video experience is intended for group viewings or individual, "one-on-one" screenings.

SPECIALIST VS. GENERALIST

When it comes to knowledge of either the audience or the subject matter, nonbroadcast scriptwriters may be specialists or generalists. As a rule, specialists treat highly technical subjects in medicine, science or engineering. Consultants may also be specialists in employee benefits or compensation communications, for instance. Corporate staff writers are more likely to be generalists, capable of tackling a variety of technical, marketing, product, financial and human resource topics.

---

[1] "Meclomen: A Unique Compound" was written by William Van Nostran, directed by James G. Libby and produced by the O'Hara Company for Parke-Davis. "Update on Hyperlipidemias" was written by Uli Monaco, directed by Bernie Boroson and produced by the Network for Continuing Medical Education. "The Perfect Serious $ Solution" was written and produced by William Van Nostran and directed by James G. Libby for Dean Witter Reynolds and Crum & Forster Corporation. "Cash & Accounts" was written, directed and produced by Jack Pignatello for Crum & Forster Corporation.

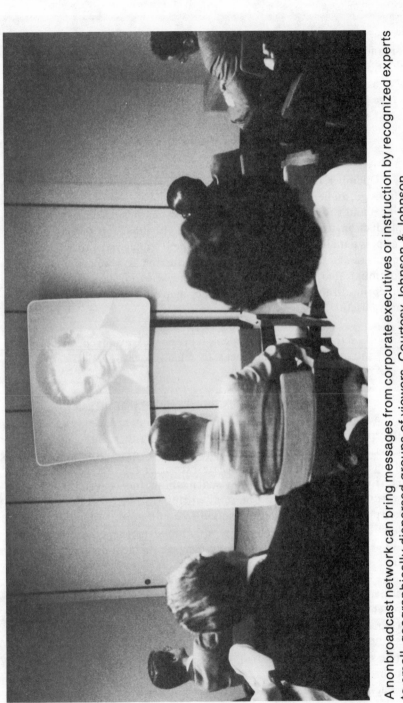

A nonbroadcast network can bring messages from corporate executives or instruction by recognized experts to small, geographically dispersed groups of viewers. Courtesy Johnson & Johnson.

Writers with staff positions work in the day-to-day environment of an organization and probably appreciate the nuances of subject matter in relation to a particular audience more quickly than an outside freelance writer. The freelance writer, however, brings fresh perspectives and a wider range of exerience to nonbroadcast assignments.

THE TELEVISION SCRIPT

Remember, the television writer fashions a *viewing* experience. To reach the target audience, the scriptwriter's words on paper need to be realized as sights and sounds. Only the client, subject matter experts and television production team *read* the writer's work. In this context, the television script is a multi-purpose working document. It has value to the client as a means of determining in advance of production how well content is being communicated. And the script serves the production team as a road map or blueprint. In analyzing this multi-functional writing task, a definition may prove useful:

> A script is a chronological sequence of events describing sounds, pictures and ideas in television production terminology.

A "chronological sequence of events" implies that the television writer communicates through a medium in which content unfolds as action in time and space. These are the dimensions the writer works within. So the television writer must develop a sense for how descriptions of "sounds, pictures and ideas" on paper translate into screen time and action. Further, television is often described as a visual medium. Indeed it is. But television is also an aural medium. The total writing task involves describing the interplay between picture and sound to communicate ideas. Finally, to function as a useful tool for the production team, the writer must use the language of television production: long shot, medium shot, close-up, zoom, sound effect and so on.

We'll refer back to this definition as we examine the three steps in the script generation process. The first phase takes the writer from research to content. In phase two, the writer evolves a concept of how the finished program will communicate content. The final phase produces a comprehensive shooting script. This book's overall approach focuses on the three-step process, illustrated with sample writings from a range of nonbroadcast situations.

Each stage in the process involves specific activities, and these activities result in a written document that serves as a checkpoint for writer, client and producer/director. Later chapters focus on techniques to insure the content of a script is on target for its objectives. We'll explore how the makeup of a specific viewing audience influences style and tone and look at various ways to structure content for television, communicating ideas through a combination of sight and sound. We'll discuss why television script formats are ideally suited to the needs of the production team yet are often confusing to the client/content expert.

With variations, the process outlined in this book can be applied to any nonbroadcast writing assignment. Use of these techniques, however, does not guarantee success. (A thorough grounding in English usage and basic narrative style is essential for any professional writing.) Television writing is, after all, more art than science; nonbroadcast television writing, more craft than science.

THE NOVICE WRITER

In nonbroadcast environments, many find scriptwriting chores thrust upon them. The nonbroadcast writer is frequently drafted from departments such as public relations, internal communications or training. These writers are apt to be print-oriented and may find their skills are not directly transferrable to television writing. The capacity to visualize and to collaborate distinguishes scriptwriting from expository print writing. Knowledge of television production techniques and practices is also essential. What the scriptwriter visualizes in the mind's eye must be realistic in terms of production facilities, budgets, people and time. Usually the nonbroadcast writer is limited in one or more of these areas. The writer must learn to maximize visual concepts so that what the script calls for is both effective and possible.

Developing these scriptwriting skills is more like learning to master a musical instrument than, say, learning to ride a bicycle. Bike riding, though it may take several tries, is mastered almost instantaneously. Once mastered, the skill stays for life. Mastering the craft of nonbroadcast television writing, however, entails disciplined practice over months and years to develop and hone skills. The craft is never completely learned, for there are always new levels of competency to strive for. Confidence is built slowly, one script at a time. Each nonbroadcast writing assignment represents a new learning opportunity.

Writers who accept the challenge and discipline of this specialized creative process should be heartened that the nonbroadcast writing market is coming of age. Already, employment possibilities are probably more numerous than in the broadcast field. And the nonbroadcast job market isn't just New York or Los Angeles. It's Dallas, Moline, Seattle, Philadelphia—wherever there are corporate offices, hospitals, universities, government agencies. Salaries and freelance fees don't match the lush pastures of prime time broadcast writing. (See Appendix A for information on job markets and salaries.) But the new technologies that created the nonbroadcast market will proliferate and mature throughout the 1980s.

The Information Age will radically alter the relationship between Americans and their television sets—in the home, at school and at work. This Information Age market will dramatically increase the demand from specialized, homogeneous audiences for video communications that will instruct, inform and motivate, as well as entertain. That's what nonbroadcast writing is all about.

2

How Television Works

INTRODUCTION

Although this book focuses on writing the nonbroadcast script, certain universal characteristics of the television medium are always at play. Nonbroadcast writers are bound by the same technical and aesthetic considerations as broadcast writers. Both should be equally conversant with the physical and psychological attributes of the medium and how these affect communication of content. In addition, the nonbroadcast writer deals with other technical considerations. Distribution methods, playback equipment and the viewing dynamics of television in educational, institutional and industrial settings are quite distinct from broadcast TV. The video cassette spurred the rapid growth of private television networks in the 1970s, and the video disc is touted today as the preferred distribution/ playback medium for interactive computer-assisted learning programs.

A comprehensive analysis of the medium, TV production techniques or even video playback equipment is beyond the scope of this book. (Books devoted to television production are listed in the Bibliography. Those readings, combined with practical production experience, are a must if you're serious about writing well for television.) However, to establish a common denominator for understanding the medium in nonbroadcast settings, this chapter examines fundamental characteristics of the television medium as well as distribution/playback equipment. We'll compare television to other media found in education, industry and government: synchronized sound/slide shows and motion pictures. What makes television different? What are the strengths and weaknesses of television in relation to slides or films? Does video cassette/ video disc technology have an impact on the application of the medium to nonbroadcast situations?

9

TELEVISION AS A MEDIUM

Television Is an Electronic Medium

Watching television differs from watching motion pictures and slides in two respects. First, motion picture and slide images are created photographically. The pure television image, by contrast, is created electronically. Further, film and slides are generally displayed by projecting and enlarging the image onto a screen. Despite the advent of video projection systems, television is most often viewed on a cathode ray tube.

Television works by converting light and dark picture values into corresponding electrical values. The picture consists of high-speed electrons, each producing a luminous spot on a cathode ray tube, organized in rows of horizontal lines known as scan lines. A complete image is composed of 525 scan lines. Thirty times per second, a complete frame, or image, is captured by these high-speed electrons.

The important consideration for the writer is not so much electronics as the psychological effects of this electronic picture on the audience. The live, happening-as-you-watch look of television is quite different from film. Watch, for example, the difference in the texture of a soap opera scene, a pure video image, compared to an episode of *Dallas*, which is shot on film, then transferred to video tape. This is not to imply that one texture is preferable to another; only that, indeed, there is a difference: the film image is created photographically; the TV image, electronically. Psychologically, television images are perceived as live pictures—even when the audience knows they're watching a video tape playback!

This live quality accounts for television's ability to convey personality with a sense of immediacy. To the over-extended executive, television offers a way of communicating in a highly personal manner. Watching people on television is like sharing time with them. (This accounts for "elevator recognition"—employees saying hello to executives whom they have actually seen only on television.) From a psychological standpoint, film does not deliver a corresponding sense of intimacy. Film's photographic image is generally projected onto a bigger-than-life screen. It is viewed in total darkness by large groups. Thus, motion pictures hold the potential for more theatrical impact than television, and the medium is capable of conveying a sense of visual reality that is compelling in its own right.

The point here is for the writer to develop a sensitivity to the texture and look of both film and television. All too often, decisions to shoot film or tape are based on economic or logistic considerations rather than the psychological or aesthetic effect one seeks for the communication. Scriptwriters, of all people, should know better.

Television Is a Motion Medium

Television and film are most alike in depicting motion. Although film and tape are actually composed of individual still frames (24 per second in film; 30 per second in video), the eye perceives the progression of stills as continuous motion. Slide shows and film strips, by contrast, are limited to displays of still images. Granted, motion is an element of computer-programmed multi-projector slide shows. But big screen multi-image productions are designed almost exclusively for theatrical, motivational presentations to large audiences. Multi-image is simply not suited to the wide range of informational, instructional and personal communications which are the staples of corporate, educational and institutional programming.

Motion, then, is a prime strength of film and television. The writer must develop scripts that realize the potential of motion to illustrate relationships. This is especially important for the nonbroadcast writer, who is often dealt inherently static subject matter. The talking head, for example, though nominally a moving image, can be an especially lifeless viewing experience. The full potential of the medium goes unrealized when opportunities to use moving images are left unexplored.

Television Is an Audio-Visual Medium

In a television presentation, content unfolds in an ever-changing mosaic of interrelated picture and sound. The combination of pictures with music, sound effects and the spoken word should result in a viewing experience greater than the sum of its parts. Developing the conceptual writing skills that focus on the ideal marriage of picture and soundtrack is the crux of writing well for television.

Television Is a Close-Up, Personal Medium

ABC Sports coined the phrase "Up Close and Personal" to profile Olympic athletes. This phrase is an apt description of television itself. The typical TV screen measures about 24 inches diagonally, several times smaller than even a modest film or slide screen. In group viewing situations, one 24-inch monitor will accommodate about 20 people. If the audience exceeds 20 people, those farthest from the single monitor will feel less involved in the viewing experience. Detailed visuals will become illegible. This is why multiple monitors are useful for audiences larger than about 20 people.

Because of this small screen, television thrives on the close-up shot—a head-and-shoulders shot of one person fills the TV frame aesthetically. Shots of two or more people speaking require judicious framing by the director to compose a satisfactory picture. Larger groups must be shot with extreme finesse and frequent intercutting of close-ups to translate well to the small screen. While television, like film, makes use of the wide, establishing shot as well as the medium view of a scene, the payoff shot is not the sweeping panorama; it's the close-up. Television scripts contain many more close-ups than medium or long shots.

Television Is a 3 x 4 "Sideways" Medium

Slides can be displayed vertically as well as horizontally. The television picture, however, is always horizontal—always 3 times high by 4 times wide. This height to width relationship, known as aspect ratio, means television graphics must always be composed for a 3 x 4 horizontal format, even for material that is inherently vertical. Television offers great flexibility in other respects, but, when it comes to aspect ratio, it's a totally rigid medium.

Television Incorporates Other Media

We've pointed out ways in which television differs from film and slides. Yet television also accommodates both these media quite well. Frequently, film, slides and artwork are used to satisfy television's voracious appetite for visual input. The photographic images of film and slides can easily be integrated into a television presentation through equipment known as a film chain. Special film or slide projectors direct the photographic image into a video camera for transfer to video tape. Of course, any slides must be horizontal and not too detailed for the reason that follows.

Television Is Not a Detail Medium

Two attributes of television combine to account for its most glaring weakness: limitation in displaying detail. This is a result first of the scan line system of dots used to generate the electronic television image. Figure 2.1, a magnified view of scan lines, demonstrates how images are resolved by the television system. The large letter has good resolution because it is composed of more scan lines. As letter height diminishes, fewer scan lines are available to convey detail. Resolution deteriorates. The second factor is television's relatively small screen. Together they demand that television graphics be bold and simple.

Obviously, writers are not responsible for the design and production of

Figure 2.1 A depiction of how television images are created by luminous spots organized in rows or horizontal scan lines. This magnified artist's rendition demonstrates why resolution deteriorates when visual content is too small or detailed. The large letter "A" has good resolution because it's composed of more scan lines. As letter size diminishes, resolution deteriorates. The lesson for writers: think in terms of bold graphics and limit the amount of text to appear on the screen. Drawing by John Onuschak.

TV graphics. But neither should the writer paint the graphic artist and director into a corner by suggesting use of graphic material that is simply too complex or detailed for resolution by the television system. For example, material that reads clearly as a slide projected on a screen may become illegible when displayed on television. Because nonbroadcast television subjects are often complex, even highly technical, the writer often has to simplify complex graphics such as detailed financial data, text or line drawings.

VIDEO PLAYBACK SYSTEMS

The characteristics of the television medium we've discussed apply equally to broadcast and nonbroadcast television. Now, let's look at the distribution and playback systems using video tape, video cassette and video disc, which have special relevance to the nonbroadcast writer.

In broadcast television's so-called golden days, virtually everything was live. But the advent of video tape recording in 1956 made it possible to record, play back and rebroadcast the electronic television signal. The resulting picture retained television's live texture and quality. Even more significant, recording on video tape offered instantaneous playback. No more taking dailies to a lab (often at some ungodly hour), having them run through the "soup" and waiting till morning to see if footage was properly exposed and in focus.

Concurrently, in the early 1960s, universities pioneered several uses of video tape recording technology in education. Instantaneous playback meant video tape could be used in the classroom as a diagnostic and feedback tool. In subjects like public speaking, students could observe and critique their own performances in a single period. This use of video tape replays also found its way into corporate classrooms for analysis of sales training role plays. In medicine, the instantaneous playback feature made video tape ideal for certain diagnostic applications, including psychological counselling and role playing.

Meanwhile, broadcast television continued to refine video tape technology. Early video recording was primitive compared to today's standards. The tape was wide; the equipment, bulky and nonportable; editing, unheard of. The first video tape editors emulated their film counterparts. If razor blades and tape worked for film, why not for video tape? Today video recording is done on highly portable equipment that offers outstanding engineering specs and reliability. The razor blade has given way to computerized video editing suites, where video tape is edited electronically with frame-to-frame accuracy comparable to film splicing.

Impact of the Video Cassette

The technological advance that gave the greatest momentum to nonbroadcast television arrived in 1972, when Sony Corp. introduced the ¾-inch U-Matic video cassette recorder and player in the United States. Their marketing plan: penetrate the industrial and educational markets.

The video cassette brought push-button technology to video tape playback. Previously even compact ½-inch reel-to-reel players/recorders had required a certain amount of technical know-how to operate. Tape had to be threaded manually. Compatibility was also a problem. Tapes recorded on one ½-inch machine would not always play back on another machine. Head clogs were common. The business executive or professor of English literature tended to doubt video tape's reliability.

The video cassette changed all that, as much for psychological as technological reasons. By housing the tape inside a cassette and automating threading, Sony demystified the process. Video cassette playback now seemed as simple as audio cassettes. The ¾-inch video cassette player also brought compatibility, reliability and a high quality color picture to video tape playback. Suddenly, managers in plants and branch offices, physicians and nurses in hospitals and clinics, teachers in the classroom all felt comfortable with this form of video tape playback.

As a result, nonbroadcast private television networks began to proliferate among corporations and organizations with decentralized operations and a need to communicate among offices and facilities located around the country. Producing television programming at headquarters and distributing video cassette copies to branch offices equipped with cassette playback hardware provided a highly efficient delivery system for personal communications. An executive could make an appearance in 12, 20, 50 or 100 cities all on the same day via video cassette. Trainers and personnel administrators were also quick to see the potential of the video cassette as a training aid.

As might be expected, this early network-building phase was hardware-oriented. Many programs were produced without scripts or written by the content expert or a print-oriented journalist. Today there is a far greater awareness that making the most of the medium begins with concepts, not equipment.

The same ease of use and reliability that made ¾-inch cassettes so successful has now been incorporated into ½-inch video cassette players. However, partly because ½-inch cassettes were originally aimed at the home market, two separate formats have been developed, VHS and Beta. Despite the resulting problems of incompatibility, the ½-inch cassette has joined the ¾-inch as an integral part of the nonbroadcast scene. The writer

needs to be as familiar with the characteristics of cassette technology as
with the television medium itself.

The Video Cassette Player Offers Uniformity and Repeatability

Video cassette programming offers a means of delivering a uniform,
consistent message throughout a large, decentralized and geographically
dispersed organization. The message can be repeated as often as necessary—
today, tomorrow, next month. For subjects such as orientation, benefits
briefings or patient information, the video cassette frees people from
having to deliver repetitive messages time and again.

The Video Cassette Player Is Multi-Functional

Today's generation of video cassette equipment offers a variety of
playback functions which are useful to nonbroadcast users. Features such
as still frame and fast forward are especially valuable in classroom and
programmed instruction applications. An automatic continuous play
feature is designed for point-of-purchase or trade show situations where
equipment is left unattended. Dual audio channels permit two separate
sound tracks to accompany the same visuals. This feature enhances
international communication, where an English track is carried on one
audio channel and a foreign language translation on the second.

The Video Cassette Encourages Interaction

Television, unlike film or slides, can be viewed in a fully lighted room.
This, combined with video cassette push-button technology, provides an
ideal interactive training environment. Students can stop the video tape
and proceed effortlessly to a classroom activity, a workbook exercise or a
simulation. Instructional designers have been quick to seize on the
possibilities of combining video with other offline learning activities for
subjects that lend themselves to programmed instruction, from computer
science to insurance coverage to product knowledge.

Instruction Goes to the Student's Location

With the video cassette, learning takes place at the student's convenience.
Employees can receive training without being taken off the job for travel to
central classrooms. Furthermore, it becomes possible to provide training
without the constant presence of an instructor. After a brief introduction

to the video cassette playback equipment, the employee, student or physician can work at his/her own pace.

Video Discs

The video disc represents the newest generation of video playback technology, though it remains to be seen how large a factor the disc will become in the nonbroadcast market.

Video Disc Technology

The video disc is like a video version of the long-playing record. Two disc technologies are currently competing in the marketplace. The more exotic is the optical system employing a grooveless disc and light from a low-powered laser. The more conventional approach involves a grooved disc and a capacitance stylus.

The disc is a playback-only piece of equipment; presently it does not record. However, it does offer the potential for low-cost mass production of large quantities of a program through the economies of scale that disc pressings make possible. The implications for the home video market are enormous and have been well reported in the trade press.

Interactive Applications

The disc offers the same advantages mentioned above for cassettes. Additionally, it permits precise, speedy random access to every individual frame it has stored. In the nonbroadcast market, this has aroused particular interest in combining the disc with a computer for use in interactive training. Using random access, instructional programs can be designed so that the computer determines the next step in the process— where to go on the disc—according to the learner's responses. Instruction is individualized, and the learner is fully involved. We'll look at interactive video in more depth in Chapter 11.

So far, disc applications have been limited in scope and impact. This technology will surely mature in the 1980s, but it remains to be seen whether the disc will replace or simply supplement the video cassette.[1]

---

[1] For more information on video discs and the uses of interactive video, see *Video Discs: The Technology, the Applications and the Future*, by Efrem Sigel, et al. (White Plains, NY: Knowledge Industry Publications, Inc., 1980) and *Handbook of Interactive Video*, edited by Steve and Beth Floyd (White Plains, NY: Knowledge Industry Publications, Inc., 1982.)

SUMMARY

In sum, television is the base medium. Nonbroadcast programs are still television shows. The characteristics that make television a unique medium are at play no matter what the application or delivery system. The emergence of a wide-scale nonbroadcast television market in business, medicine and education has resulted from advances in the technology of delivery systems—how television pictures get recorded, duplicated, distributed and played back. The writer must be familiar with the attributes of the television medium and of the distribution playback systems. Both have an impact on the ultimate design of nonbroadcast television programming.

3

Research Techniques:
Getting to the Sources

Nonbroadcast television communications are initiated by clients who expect the medium to do something for them. The writer is called in to design and script a television program to satisfy individual client needs. The nonbroadcast market is for custom communications aimed at a highly defined audience. Research is how the writer—whether staff or free-lance—comes to understand and appreciate each client's unique and specific needs.

Research is sometimes intimidating because nonbroadcast television subject matter can prove intimidating. Remember these program titles?

"Meclomen: A Unique Compound"
"Update on Hyperlipidemias"
"The Perfect Serious $ Solution"
"Cash & Accounts"

These titles suggest highly technical subjects, complex business or economic issues, medical and educational curricula. By and large, these subjects cannot be researched through material that is publicly available. It takes access to inside information that must be pieced together by talking with content specialists. Furthermore, in the nonbroadcast field, research may go beyond the content or subject matter of the video presentation. In many situations, it's equally important to develop an appreciation of your client's total communication or training environment. Knowledge of the audience's likely attitude toward the topic, the logistics of the viewing environment and even cultural attitudes within an organization all yield insights which become invaluable once it's time to decide on program format, style and tone.

Although research is always the first step in the writing process, specific research activities vary widely from project to project. A field trip may be essential for one project and totally inappropriate for the next. Interviews with the target audience may generate valid input for treating some topics yet be superfluous in other instances. The research task facing the nonbroadcast writer can be quite substantial. And it's not uncommon to conduct research under deadline pressure.

The writer needs solid research methods: a system that yields comprehensive data, yet is also efficient and flexible. This chapter outlines such a research method—one that can be applied equally well to different situations.

THE CORE QUESTION

For any nonbroadcast project, the goal of all research activities is to develop an answer to one fundamental question. We'll call it the core question. It goes like this:

What do you want to say, to whom, and for what purpose?

Answers to the core question fall into one of three categories of information:

1. "What do you want to say..." provides information relevant to the *content* of the television communication.

2. "To whom..." focuses on the *audience* for the finished program.

3. "For what purpose..." gives the writer an understanding of *objectives*—what the program intends to accomplish.

There are many ways to get at an answer to this question. Obviously, a comprehensive answer can become more detailed than your finished shooting script. Research activities often span several weeks involving meetings with many individuals, site surveys to observe activities firsthand and, of course, a certain amount of reading. Finally, when client and writer agree on answers to that core question, it's time to move from researching to writing.

THE RESEARCH AGENDA

The research agenda offers a method of coming to grips with the complexities of each assignment. Through the research agenda, the writer formulates a specific plan of attack for gathering both the hard data and the psychological insights necessary to proceed to more conceptual work. The research agenda identifies and itemizes specific steps that will be taken to gather input on content, audience and objectives. Typically, the research agenda can include activities such as:

- Interviews—a listing of content experts or members of the target audience you must talk with to gain their insights and viewpoints on the project.

- Observations—those physical locations or processes you must see to gain knowledge of the visual possibilities inherent in the content.

- Readings—those sources, often primary ones, that you need as reference material.

We'll proceed through the major steps in the research agenda and discuss techniques for conducting interviews and field observations, as well as points to consider in using reference material.

Getting an Overview

To formulate a research agenda, the writer needs an overview perspective on the program's proposed content, audience and objectives. Usually, this information is gained from an initial research session with the client and possibly one or more content experts. Others involved in such initial sessions could include the show's producer and director. In this first meeting you're seeking a big picture answer to the core question: "What do you want to say, to whom, for what purpose?" Guard against bogging down in details on content, audience or objectives. Focus instead on developing a sense of the total communication/training task. For now, your interview technique should be exploratory and open-ended, encouraging the client to discuss the rationale for doing the program as well as the subject matter itself.

Probe with questions that relate to elements of the core question, beginning with "What do you want to say?" Fortunately, you'll find the client usually answers in general terms at first. For example:

- We want a program to explain the benefits of a tax-deferred annuity as an investment...

- Our blood gas analyzer product is facing increasing competition in the marketplace, so we want to show why our product remains the best...

- In the last several years, a new international seizure classification system has been adopted by the medical community for diagnosing and treating epileptic patients. This program will explain that classification system...

Often, there's a temptation to jump into details right away. Resist. Ask only those follow-up questions that are essential for you to comprehend the client's statement of content. If you haven't the vaguest idea what blood gas analyzer products are all about, now's the time to find out more. But don't press for detailed content until you get a complete description of the assignment.

Once you've got the idea of the subject matter in general, go directly to the next part of the question.

What do you want to say, *to whom*...

Remember, the nonbroadcast television program is always targeted to a specific viewing audience. The composition of that audience, their predisposition to the subject, the viewing environment—all these factors bear significantly on the writer's ultimate creative strategy. So, during this initial interview look for a basic description of the audience.

Following the initial examples a step further, the client may tell you:

- We want to explain the benefits of a tax-deferred annuity investment *to potential investors*...

- Our blood gas analyzer product is facing more and more competitive products, so we want to show why our product is still the best on the market. The program will be seen by our *field sales force*...

- In the last several years, a new international seizure classification system has been adopted by the medical community for diagnosing and treating epileptic patients. This program will explain that classification system *to physicians*...

A specific target audience in each case: potential investors, a field sales force, physicians. By viewing subject matter or content in the context of the intended audience, the writer learns a great deal about the nature of the research and writing assigment. Change the audience for any of the case study examples, and you face an entirely different communication environment.

- We want to explain the benefits of a tax-deferred annuity to *our firm's brokers* in field offices...

- Our blood gas analyzer product is facing increasing competition in the marketplace, so we want to show why our product remains the best. The program will be shown to *potential customers* at a trade show...

Even though the content is unchanged, the nature of the communication or training task changes radically based on the client's intended audience. When the audience consists of sales representatives, for example, the approach to subject matter will be markedly different in both content and tone than a similar subject presented to potential customers. Beware the client who wants to address multiple audiences in a single presentation. This usually results in a presentation that lacks focus.

Depending on the writer's familiarity with the target audience, a significant portion of the research agenda may focus on gathering insight into the audience's level of knowledge or attitudes. Interviews with representative audience members, observation of their work activities or use of research tools such as attitude surveys are techniques the writer may find helpful for some assignments. However it's accomplished, the writer must construct a valid profile of the target audience—their current understanding of subject matter as well as their receptivity to the message.

But before getting too involved in profiling the audience, complete the overview interview by asking about the purpose, or objective, of the program.

What do you want to say, to whom, *for what purpose?*

The answer to this final part of the core question forms the foundation for delineating program objectives. Remember, nonbroadcast television programs are generated by clients who expect the medium to do something for them. The writer's work is ultimately measured by the success of the finished program in fulfilling the client's purpose and meeting stated objectives.

In general, the most common objectives for nonbroadcast communications are to inform, to instruct, to demonstrate, to motivate. Frequently, a television communication involves multiple objectives. As with the content and audience, the writer's task in research is to arrive at a specific understanding and agreement with the client on objectives. It starts with an overview.

- We want to explain the benefits of a tax-deferred annuity to potential investors. The goal is to have the *broker close the sale* at the end of the tape.

- Our blood gas analyzer product is facing more and more competitive products, so we want to show why our product is still the best. The program will be seen by our own field sales force. The program should give them the ammunition *to overcome objections and misconceptions of potential customers.*

- In the last several years, a new international seizure classification system has been adopted by the medical community for diagnosing and treating epileptic patients. This program will explain the classification system to physicians and *build skills for recognizing and classifying epileptic patients by both physical observation and brain wave readings.*

With this general understanding of the program's content, audience and objectives, the writer is prepared for delving into specifics.

Establishing a Research Agenda

In simple terms, the research agenda is a listing of whom the writer must interview, what the writer should observe first-hand, and which written documents serve as reference material. A research agenda may include any or all of these components:

```
        Content research - Interviews
                           Observations
                           Readings
       Audience research - Interviews
                           Observations
                           Readings
Verification of objectives - (Ongoing throughout the
                           research agenda)
```

We'll explore these one at a time.

The research stage: a good research agenda helps the writer come to grips with the assignment. Drawing by Steven Thomas.

Content Research

Interviews

Normally, interviews are conducted with content experts—individuals with special knowledge and insight into the "what" of a communication. Many times, more than one expert will be involved in providing input, and often the client is also a content expert. Whenever possible, interview those who can provide overview material first. That way, you'll develop the proper perspective for interviews with those specialists who provide details on only a single aspect of the subject. The research agenda in Figure 3.1 refers to a project on tax-deferred annuities. Notice how the writer seeks specific points of view from each interview subject.

Figure 3.1: Sample Research Agenda: Interviews

RESEARCH AGENDA
Project: Tax-Deferred Annuity Presentation

Interviews

Subject	Point of View
Mr. Hal Gibson Product Manager	Overview

Ms. Sharon Reeves
  Advertising and Sales
  Promotion Manager
	Promotional materials available to sales reps. Probe to determine if special print pieces should be developed to support video presentation.

Mr. Jerry Rubenstein Sales Representative	Identified as top annuity sales rep. Find out his sales technique and approach to overcoming objections.
Mr. David Hartman Senior Actuary	Mr. Hartman developed product and is source for all technical/financial questions.
Mr. William Donleavy National Sales Manager	Has best insight into attitudes and needs of brokers and sales reps who will use the program. Mr. Donleavy is also a key man in implementation, so his input in that area is critical.

Begin by identifying what each person will contribute to the overall perspective. Successful interviewing involves mental preparation, concentration, listening skills and an ability to probe with follow-up questions. Of course, you'll want to ask content experts some questions simply as background. But in preparing interview questions, try to take the audience's point of view:

• How does a tax-deferred annuity compare to other popular investment options?

- What investment goals does the tax-deferred annuity fulfill best?

Questions phrased like the above are also open-ended, beginning with words like how, what or why. Because they require explanations, not a simple yes, no or maybe, open-ended questions are ideal for getting interview subjects talking in substantive detail.

Listening skills are a prime requisite of the competent interviewer. While you will prepare a list of questions in advance, interviews invariably take on a life of their own. The ability to keep probing for complete answers or to take advantage of a totally unexpected line of questioning will help you get what you need from content sources. Some interviewers are note takers; others prefer audio cassette recordings. I lean toward taking notes even while recording. You never know when gremlins may invade the tape recorder. Further, if you only have an audio recording, chances are you've got to play back the entire interview again in order to take notes. So why not work productively and listen critically just once?

In one sense, the writer functions as a surrogate researcher for the audience. In this vein, never feel inhibited about asking the content expert to clarify a fuzzy point. If *you* don't fully understand the subject, how can you explain it to the audience? Often, the audience would want to ask the identical question. Devil's advocate questioning can be a valuable interview technique and may also parallel the audience's point of view:

- Why should I invest in an annuity when there's an opportunity for a quicker killing in the stock market?

- Why should I purchase your firm's annuity product instead of a competitor's?

Such questions bring out issues that might go unexplored with less direct questions. Pursuing content from the audience's point of view is the only way to write convincingly and to make intelligent, informed recommendations about program format, style and tone.

Observations

The eye is a vital research tool of the nonbroadcast writer—eventually, you'll organize content for the eye of the audience. There are, of course, certain abstract or conceptual topics that require the writer to devise an entire visual framework from the mind. More frequently though, you need to consider the variety of visual sources that you must see to do an adequate research job. In addition to field trips, the writer should not overlook existing artwork, graphics, photographs, slides, film footage or other visual sources which relate to the subject. Such materials may not be suitable for integrating into the production, but find out what does exist. Consider those materials as a way of developing your own visual fluency with the topic.

Sometimes the subject matter demands personal observation. If you're writing about a manufacturing process, a new surgical technique or a new product, then it's imperative to gain firsthand visual knowledge of what's involved. What does the manufacturing process look like? (Are raw materials involved? Is there an assembly line? What role do people play in the process?) What does the new product look like? (How does it operate? What distinguishes it from competition? How do people interact with the product?) Figure 3.2 gives an example of observations scheduled in a research agenda for an orientation program on General Foods' Maxwell House Division.

Figure 3.2: Sample Research Agenda: Observations

RESEARCH AGENDA

Field Trips

1. Visit Maxwell House Houston plant to observe coffee roasting, blending and packaging processes. Emphasis should be on differences in making ground, instant, freeze-dried and decaffeinated coffees.

2. Visit Wall Street green bean buying office to observe commodity buying activity and green bean taste-testing procedures.

In doing this visual research, focus on the physical characteristics of the process or machinery and how well such visual elements can be translated to the televison screen. Learn to look for what is invisible as well as visible. If key elements of a manufacturing process are hidden from view, then animation might be considered as a means of visualizing the process. On the other hand, if you're looking at a manufacturing process where creation of the finished product occurs in clearly visible stages, then watch the process with an eye toward location shooting.

Another important consideration in observation research is the correlation between real time and screen time. Real time events often need to be condensed and compressed through editing to arrive at pacing suitable for the television viewing experience. A laboratory experiment, for example, may take hours, even days, to accomplish in real time. In researching such a process, the writer should focus on those discrete steps that are essential to the communication and fashion an explanation appropriate for television time.

In some instances, local color may be an important visual element of the communication. If your subject is an orientation to a college campus, walk the campus with an eye toward potential visual input which will help convey the character of the institution.

Bear in mind that interviewing generally accompanies this observation. Be prepared to ask questions of those who live or work in the environment each day.

One final point on observation: a camera can prove invaluable in recording visual sources for your own reference and for pre-production planning sessions with the director. Document your observations with snapshots or Polaroids.

Readings

Your research agenda should also include a listing of written sources that will serve as reference material. In gathering this material, most writers prefer too much rather than too little. These references can include published documents such as annual reports, product literature, press releases, promotional copy, training manuals, technical bulletins or benefits booklets. Often, however, the most useful written sources are more informal documents: research reports, internal memos, planning and implementation schedules, field test reports, marketing intelligence. Experience will develop the sense of inquiry needed to uncover these valuable references. Occasionally, the client or content expert plans ahead and has several pertinent documents ready and waiting for the writer. If not, ask for literature—both formal and informal source material.

Rapport and trust must be established with the client. Sometimes you will need proprietary, confidential or otherwise sensitive information as background for understanding your assignment. When sensitive subject matter is involved, good business ethics require writers to honor client requests for confidentiality.

Finally, don't overlook the library as a research source. If you're writing on an aspect of a general subject, or an extremely topical subject, the library is a good place to bone up, particularly for initial interviews. Additionally, the nonbroadcast writer can often make use of special libraries such as medical or scientific ones. Corporate headquarters sometimes contain libraries or information centers with a wealth of material pertinent to their business. Trade associations generally produce reams of material and publish periodicals and books. (There's a listing of trade associations relevant to the nonbroadcast writer in Appendix B. Most of them sponsor ongoing member communications activities.)

Audience Research

In audience research, a staff writer holds a decided edge over the freelance writer. In any environment, the staff person has greater opportunity for daily contact with the people who constitute various segments of the organizational population.

Personal knowledge of the audience is most critical when a communication is likely to meet resistance. One research objective, then, should be to determine the daily dynamics of the communication environment. When you're dealing with a negative communication environment or when the objective of the communication involves motivation or persuasion, then firsthand knowledge of the audience, their opinions and their attitudes is extremely valuable. And because an approach which generates enthusiasm in one organization could sound paternalistic in another, the tone of the communication and your motivational appeals becomes increasingly important.

Interviewing representative audience members is one way to develop the psychological insight necessary to present content effectively. Go about the selection process in the same manner as for content interviews. Devise a research agenda indicating whom you should talk to and what unique perspective they bring to the subject. Be sure to set the proper tone for audience interviews at the outset. If you're interviewing hourly employees, for instance, bear in mind they will perceive you as a management representative. You must gain their trust and establish rapport in order to elicit anything more than the most superficial responses.

For some topics, observation of the audience may be more relevant than interviewing. If the subject involves training or the operation of specific equipment, observe an operator in action and ask questions as appropriate. Also, don't abandon the devil's advocate line of questioning. Seek honesty and spontaneity in these sessions. When the subject is sensitive, abandon note taking or audio recording. You're not after content in these discussions; probe feelings, attitudes and individual perceptions. Avoid the tendency to lead the subject. A lengthy pause will often get a better response than a complex follow-up question.

Verification of Objectives

In researching both content and audience, keep the client's overall objective in mind. As you develop greater knowledge about the subject and the communication task, continue to analyze whether you have sufficient data to meet the client's objective. If not, either more research is required, or the objective should be reassessed. If the latter, ask whether the objective is realistic given what you know about content and audience. Can the objective be more clearly focused or broken down into partial steps? (More on the mechanics of objective setting and verification in Chapter 4.)

If you feel confident that you have the necessary data to achieve the client's objective with the target audience, it's a good indication that your research job is complete. When you begin to hear and read the same points repeated with little new information added, you can be confident that the research effort has been thorough and comprehensive.

SUMMARY

The concept of a research agenda is simply a way of bringing a structure to research activities. It's not necessary to formulate a written agenda to complete every research assignment though it probably insures better results and record keeping. More important is that you develop a research method which is both efficient and comprehensive, one that you are comfortable using, one that produces consistent results. Work to develop interviewing skills. Become an analytical, active listener. Empathize with people, especially your target audience. And use the eye, as well as the mind, when researching for a television presentation.

4

Translating Research into Action: The Audience, the Objectives and the Content Outline

"Information overload!" A typical reaction to research. You've accumulated more raw data than can possibly be crammed into a single video presentation. You feel primed for writing; there's a sense of urgency about how or where to begin. What material merits treatment in the script? How much screen time should be devoted to each topic? Which visual resources can you draw upon? What style and tone are appropriate? Do you recommend professional talent or participation of the real people involved?

Questions like these indicate you're ready for that intermediate stage between research and scriptwriting. This stage of writing may go by many names: proposal, action plan, research report, recommendations. For the next two chapters, we'll use the term "action plan." A comprehensive action plan contains at least four items:

- Audience profile
- Objectives
- Content outline
- Television treatment

By organizing research results into a format that sets down parameters for the project, you discover exactly where you're headed and how you plan to get there. Just as the shooting script functions as a blueprint for the production crew, the action plan serves as a blueprint for the scriptwriter. It's easier, and much more efficient, to develop a full-blown shooting script working from a content outline and screen treatment than from a mound of disjointed research findings, random notes and tape-recorded interviews.

More important, the action plan provides a superb checkpoint communication between writer and client. It's an ideal method of feeding back research results and verifying your understanding of the program's audience, objectives and content. It's a way of saying to the client: "This is what I heard you and others involved in the project say you wanted. Did I hear you correctly?" Usually, the client finds areas requiring a slightly different focus: an oversight in content, a shift of emphasis here and there.

The action plan also provides an ideal format for introducing creative ideas in the television treatment. Once agreed to by the client, this document forms a contract between writer and client, a go-ahead to proceed as planned. Finally, the action plan allows the producer/director to respond to the writer's presentational thrust. From the content outline and the television treatment, the director can begin to structure the program as a production. The director is also likely to make suggestions that enhance the creative concept. Good television results from close collaboration.

In short, the action plan lets client, producer and director know just what the writer has learned from research and where the project is headed substantively and creatively.

In this chapter, we'll discuss writing the first three elements of the action plan: audience profile, objectives and content outline. Only after clarifying these items on paper should the writer pursue the concepts and visualizations needed to develop a television treatment. These creative concepts will best evolve from a consideration of audience, objectives and content. The visualization process will be taken up in Chapter 5.

THE AUDIENCE PROFILE

Writing descriptions of the target audience is often overlooked in the development of a project. After all, you may reason, doesn't the client know the target audience better than the writer? Why expend effort on feeding back what the client already knows? Quite simply, understanding your audience is so crucial to the writer's ultimate selection of a program format, style and tone, that it's absolutely essential to gain agreement from the client on the characteristics of the audience. For instance, given the same content, you'd write quite differently for an audience that views the message as good news compared to one that is likely to be negative, even hostile, toward the communication. If your writing task involves motivating an audience, then the program must contain appeals that are meaningful to that audience. If the program involves instruction, you'll need to understand the audience's initial knowledge of the subject matter and their likely motivation to learn.

Internal and External Audiences

In broad terms, your communication will usually go to either an internal or external audience. Internal audiences may consist of employees, staff members of hospitals or institutions or members of a professional group. A video program introducing a new product to a national sales force, for example, typifies the internal communication. The writer's point of view focuses on what the sales force needs to know to sell the product successfully.

Introducing that same new product to potential buyers involves an external communication and requires a different perspective and point of view. External audiences are public audiences—customers, patients, government officials, financial analysts. The writer not only conveys information but presents an image of the organization to outsiders. That image should be consistent with an organization's overall public relations posture.

Determining whether you're writing for an internal or an external audience provides an initial handle on the perspective to take in shaping the material. Then come more subtle audience characteristics.

Establishing the Profile

For any project, the target audience may not always be a homogeneous group but may include secondary and sometimes tertiary audience segments. Even a seemingly homogeneous group, such as a company's sales force, is likely to consist of grizzled veterans alongside eager recruits. Each may respond to identical content in different ways. A single television presentation cannot be all things to all people.

For these reasons, a useful audience profile contains more than a two-word description such as sales representatives, new employees, security analysts or physicians and nurses. Those are generic occupational classifications, not profiles of a clearly perceived target audience characterized by common attributes and shared motivations. Strive instead for a description of the audience that lets the client know you appreciate the nuances of the audience's makeup.

For instance, take a look at this audience profile for an internal video project. The program involves a video announcement for a new and massive national television advertising campaign to beef up sales for an over-the-counter multiple vitamin product.

The audience is the pharmaceutical sales force. During the past 18 months, the home office has placed a priority on *physician*

> details. In this video program, we will be asking the sales force to build inventories at the *retail* pharmacy level. Unless properly positioned, the sales force could perceive this as a case of conflicting priorities and lack of coordinated direction.

Here, the writer pinpoints a characteristic of the audience that directly affects their attitude: the company's recent emphasis on physician details (pharmaceutical jargon for sales calls) as opposed to selling to the retail pharmacy. This descriptive audience profile telegraphs to the client that the writer appreciates the audience's unique point of view.

Remember, nonbroadcast television programming is directed toward audiences who share a particular interest in the subject matter. In describing a target audience, then, seek to delineate its point of view toward the subject matter.

Take a look at this next profile of an external, or public, audience. The client manufactures a line of high quality home video recording tape stock and faces a highly competitive market environment.

> This video cassette presentation will be suitable for use as a retail point-of-purchase demonstration tape with the *consumer* of blank video tape stock. For the most part, consumers of blank stock tend to base purchasing decisions primarily on price. They do not perceive nor understand that the quality of blank tape can have an effect on performance—particularly in critical applications such as slow record and playback functions or during freeze framing and rapid search modes. This audience, however, is composed of people who have made sizeable investments in home video gear and may be motivated to purchase a higher priced quality tape stock if benefits in terms of picture quality and/or machine wear can be demonstrated convincingly.

This analytical profile is much more functional to client and writer than a terse: "The audience is the consumer of blank tape stock." Through this profile, the writer tells the client that he or she has a firm grip on the psychological makeup of the audience: that consumers currently buy on the basis of price, not tape performance. To make an impact, the video demonstration will have to show benefits of a high-grade, quality blank stock. And, to round out the audience profile, the writer suggests the key to motivating this audience through appeals to their investment in video cassette hardware.

In short, the client is given sufficient feedback either to agree with the writer's perception or to correct and clarify that perception. The writer may simply be parroting back what the client has explained about the viewing audience. But there's now basis for consensus—on paper.

The Viewing Situation

In the above audience profile, the writer included information about the viewing situation. We learned that the program will be viewed at point of purchase in the hubbub of retail stores. Playback environments and their resulting psychological effects on the audience often influence writing decisions. There's a world of difference between a message that will be seen in the structured internal viewing environment of a corporate conference room and one that is seen by a random, casual public audience in a retail store. Whenever the physical viewing situation has an impact on audience psychology and response, consider a reference to that viewing situation in the audience profile.

Multiple Audiences

So far, we've looked at writing profiles for a single target audience. Frequently, the writer must address multiple audiences with a single program. For instance, suppose our client who manufactures blank tape stock has a secondary audience in mind for the presentation: the retail floor salesperson. Here's how that secondary audience might be described.

> The retail floor salesperson, unfortunately, is ill equipped to explain the differences in quality which characterize a higher priced blank tape stock. Through this presentation, the retail salesperson will receive useful product knowledge on the interface between home video recorder and blank stock through exposure to the presentation to consumers.

The writer has clearly positioned the primary and secondary audiences as separate and distinct groups. The program will speak directly to the consumer, the primary audience. The message will be absorbed by the secondary audience, the retail floor salesperson, by exposure to the program. At no time, however, will content be presented directly to the retail salesperson. In this way, the client is forewarned there are limitations in what can be communicated to the secondary audience. You couldn't, for instance, employ a theme such as "Remember, your profit margin is higher when you sell higher priced tape" in a presentation that will be shown to consumers! The secondary audience is just that—a group of viewers who will be exposed to the content, although it is not directed toward them.

If there is more than one target group, analyze whether their points of view are sufficiently diverse to affect what content can or cannot be presented to both. Whenever that situation exists, clearly identify a primary audience—the single group content will be pitched at. Then describe how the secondary audience will relate to that content.

This may seem like a lot of detail to arrive at a simple statement of the audience. But a single program cannot be all things to all people. You must be explicit in this early stage and spell out what you intend to accomplish for a client—and what cannot be accomplished.

OBJECTIVES: STATEMENTS OF EXPECTATION

Stating program objectives is about as important a piece of writing as you can do on a project. Look at it this way: objectives are expressions of what everyone with a stake in the project expects the finished product to accomplish. A program that meets stated objectives fulfills the client's expectations for the project. No matter how spectacular the production, if a program fails to deliver on objectives, it must be deemed a failure.

When the client approves a writer's list of objectives, two things occur simultaneously. Most important, expectations are established. And the client limits the scope and range of the work. In this light, objectives are as significant for what they do not state as for what they do.

If you have had any experience at all in nonbroadcast television, you have surely attended preview screenings of a completed program. Typically, the client has invited a number of cronies to sit in. Usually, these newcomers have had no involvement in the project and know little of its evolution. At the conclusion of the preview, there's a pregnant pause. Eventually, the client says simply: "That was very good. I think that's just what we need." The ice is broken. Now more insightful comments begin to surface—generally all laudatory.

Then, inevitably, one crony ventures this opinion: "You know, I thought it was fine as far as it went. But you really didn't get into the responsibility of plant engineering to provide input to R&D engineering. How come?" For the writer's sake, the answer to that question had best be: "We considered that point early on but determined that wasn't one of our objectives because. . ."

Once objectives are set down on paper, they remain operative throughout the production. And since objectives do define expectations for the program, they form the foundation for the client's ultimate evaluation of the finished product. For these reasons, the nonbroadcast writer must develop a technique for expressing the intent of each communication through a precise, realistic description of what the program can achieve. If objectives raise unrealistic expectations, it always comes back to haunt the writer. Let's look at what's involved in constructing and writing objectives.

An objective defines a change that a program is intended to effect in its viewers. Change may be as internal and subtle as a heightened awareness resulting from exposure to new information. Or the change may go further, seeking to influence the audience's attitudes or level of motivation. Most dramatically, the program may actually attempt to change overt, observable actions—people's behavior. These three generic objectives can be called informational, motivational and behavioral. If you plot the audience involvement necessary to attain these three generic types as in Figure 4.1, there's a clear movement from a rather passive, uninvolved audience to one which must become actively involved, learning new skills or concepts. And, as we'll discuss below, the degree of audience involvement directly affects the ease with which the results of a program can be measured.

Figure 4.1: Audience Involvement and Ease of Measuring Results for the Three Types of Objectives

INFORMATIONAL OBJECTIVE	MOTIVATIONAL OBJECTIVE	BEHAVIORAL OBJECTIVE
Passive audience		Active audience
←		→
Results difficult to measure		Results easy to measure

Informational Objectives

Programs designed to fill only informational objectives are usually straightforward and presentational in style. The corporate news program typifies the communication with informational objectives. Following are two examples of written informational objectives.

- To demonstrate that Acme Industries is a key supplier of material handling equipment, capable of delivering a wide range of products and systems to solve diverse industrial problems.

- To show how the test kitchens are organized to support divisional development and marketing activities for new food products.

Informational objectives do not place demands on the audience. The implication is simply that information will be presented. How the audience is expected to respond or act upon this new information is not specified.

Behavioral Objectives

On the opposite end of the continuum, however, is programming with behavioral objectives. In these instances, the audience's actions are detailed quite specifically. Since behavioral changes are observable, they can be measured through pre- and post-test devices. Changing behavior generally requires training. In fact, the behavioral objective is synonymous with the instructional objective. Video programs intended to teach or instruct should be described with behavioral objectives. As Robert Mager points out in *Preparing Instructional Objectives*, in order to instruct successfully, the program designer must state objectives in terms of the terminal behavior expected of the learner; that is, "an objective always states a performance, describing what the learner will be DOING when demonstrating mastery of the objective."[1]

Here are examples of behavioral objectives for video-based training programs:

- Upon completion of this program, the trainee will be able to type, store, recall and modify correspondence, reports, forms and other materials using features of the WP201 Word Processor.

- At the conclusion of this instructional unit, participants will be able to identify and classify epileptic seizures using the International Classification System based on patient observation and analysis of brain wave recordings.

Different as these two program topics and objectives are, both contain the phrase "will be able to." By stating what the viewer or learner will be able to

---

[1] Robert Mager, *Preparing Instructional Objectives*, second edition. (Belmont, CA: Pitman Learning Inc., 1975) p.48.

do after completing the program, you identify the expected terminal behavior.

Of course, the behavioral objectives above are overall course objectives. To reach the overall objective, the student must master a multitude of limited and specific subobjectives that function as necessary component building blocks. Here are several subobjectives taken from a gas turbine training program for operators and maintenance personnel.

> To achieve the overall objective, content and exercises will be structured so that participants *will be able to:*
>
> • Identify basic turbine components: gas generator, HP compressor drive turbine, LP turbine, load.
>
> • Demonstrate an understanding of the use of control parameters to protect gas turbine parts.
>
> • Identify various control systems used to overcome air compressor stall.
>
> • Select an appropriate course of action when high temperatures are present.

In all, there are 36 subobjectives for this particular training module. Each is stated in behavioral terms and contributes to mastery of the overall course objective.

Behavioral or instructional objectives require that the learner become sufficiently involved in the content of training programs to demonstrate the desired behavior. Instructional programming, therefore, often uses interactive techniques, allowing the learner to stop the video presentation and practice with workbook exercises, simulations, role playing, quizzes and other activities. Writers developing video programming for educational or instructional purposes should bone up on the function and form of instructional objectives and the principles of interactive media-based training. We'll return to the subject of interactive video in Chapter 11. See also Robert Mager's books on setting objectives, which are listed in the Bibliography. For now, the important point is that objectives for instructional programming must be stated in behavioral terms, describing *how* the learner will demonstrate achievement of the objective.

Motivational Objectives

The motivational objective stands between the two extremes of informational and behavioral objectives. The terminal behavior for motivational objectives is less specific than for instructional objectives, yet a definite response to subject matter is sought. For instance, take a typical corporate video communication topic: the annual report to employees. When the company is coming off a good year, the report may be purely informational, stressing positive developments in sales, operations and markets. In a year of poor performance, however, the emphasis may shift to more motivational objectives, such as:

- To stress the need for budgetary restraint in all areas of operations.

- To improve manufacturing productivity by reducing material waste and manufacturing defects.

- To create a greater awareness of the role of interdepartmental communication in improving customer service.

Here the audience must be persuaded to adopt an attitude that will then translate into more specific behaviors as conditions dictate. This makes the motivational program more difficult to conceive and execute than either the informational or training program. Appeals will often be emotional as well as intellectual. Furthermore, measuring the results of such programming is difficult. How does one measure subjective attitudes such as "greater awareness of the role of interdepartmental communication in improving customer services"? Motivational objectives often lack definitive criteria. How *much* budgetary restraint is needed, for instance? Or *how* can production workers reduce waste and manufacturing defects? These objectives are wide open to individual interpretation.

When the writer is assigned a program with motivational objectives, good judgment is needed to insure objectives are realistic. Management may expect too much from a single motivational communication. During the objective-setting stage, then, the writer should seek to clarify what the video presentation can and cannot accomplish. Granted, television is a useful medium to create awareness and raise major issues. It may be an appropriate vehicle to explore the role of interdepartmental communication in improving customer service. But to have an actual effect on customer service, management may need to streamline work flow procedures or improve productivity through a computerized order system. Raising unrealistic expectations for a video presentation is a disservice to all involved: the client, the production team, the medium itself.

In summary, then, whatever the subject, most video projects revolve around the three generic types of objectives. Moving from informational to behavioral objectives requires greater audience involvement in program content. Consequently, it's easier to measure the results of programming with behavioral objectives than with motivational and informational programming. When defining program objectives, the writer must be aware of which category of generic objective is involved.

All objectives direct effort toward an end. Use of the directive word "to" is a convenient way to insure objectives point toward an end result. Read through the sample objectives in this chapter and notice how the directive "to" functions in each. Finally, bear in mind that in order to achieve an overall program objective, several subobjectives must be accomplished. It's not unusual for a single program to contain informational, motivational and behavioral objectives. After all, one must impart information in order to instruct; and one must often motivate the learner to become actively involved.

Whatever the writing assignment, take the time to state program objectives with clarity and precision. Remember, you're establishing expectations for the program. As Mager advises: "What we are searching for is that group of words or symbols that will communicate your intent exactly as YOU understand it." [2]

THE CONTENT OUTLINE

The third element in the action plan is a comprehensive content outline. The outline excerpt in Figure 4.2 presents content points for an instructional video tape on the features and benefits of a quality control product used in hospital diagnostic laboratories to verify the calibration and accuracy of blood gas instruments. The audience here consists of sales trainees. Note that the outline includes space for client comments. The outline provides another important checkpoint between writer and client. Look for clues to how the writer intends to treat this material as a television presentation.

If you failed to pick up on anything which characterizes this outline as specifically written for television, that's good. There's nothing to distinguish a content outline for a video presentation from an outline for any other medium. The purpose of the content outline is to focus attention solely on what the program is going to be about, and it should intentionally avoid matters of style, format or special effects. Given identical audience descriptions, objectives and research findings, five different writers should arrive at quite similar content outlines. In treating the material for the

---

[2]Ibid., p. 19.

Figure 4.2: Sample Content Outline
INTRODUCTION

VIDEO TAPE CONTENT	CLIENT COMMENTS

I. Product/market overview

   A. Product integrity—General Diagnostics offers best blood gas analyzer quality control product on the market. Claim backed by experience and third party endorsements.

   B. Ease of use—Product stores conveniently. Test procedures simple to follow. Designed for use on all blood gas instruments.

   C. Services—General Diagnostics offers widest range of useful, comprehensive support services.

II. In light of this, how can competition be penetrating the market with inferior products and services?

   A. Product features are not perceived as benefits by the customer.

      1. Example: A less sensitive product may give the lab a false sense of confidence in their instruments.

      2. Example: Statistical data may be meaningless to a customer who cannot interpret raw data.

      3. Example: Customer may not appreciate need for accurate values at different levels.

   B. These and other typical objections can be overcome through customer education.

[Handwritten client comments in the right margin:] THIS IS A KEY COMPETITIVE ADVANTAGE. I HOPE YOU PLAN TO ELABORATE ON THIS LATER.

[Handwritten client comments:] PERCEPTION IS THE KEY POINT HERE. THE ISSUE OF QC PRODUCTS UTILIZING HUMAN BLOOD IS ANOTHER IMPORTANT EXAMPLE OF HOW MISCONCEPTIONS IN THE MARKETPLACE WILL AFFECT SALES. YOU MUST ADDRESS THAT ISSUE!

---

screen, however, these five writers are likely to be totally different and distinctive in style, tone and approach. One might employ humor; another, dramatization; still a third, an elaborate stage setting in order to present identical content.

That's why the content outline should be written after the writer has formulated the audience profile and the objectives and prior to writing a television treatment. The audience profile and the statement of objectives form a matrix that helps the writer identify what content needs to be communicated to the audience in order to reach the stated objectives. In reviewing research findings, begin by relating the content to the audience and objectives. Information that helps achieve an objective should be included in the content outline. Use traditional formatting and organizational techniques to arrive at the video content outline. If the subject matter lends itself to a chronological ordering, use that sequence. If a topical or cause and effect structure makes sense, then go that route. This does not mean that the content will follow in identical order in the television script. That decision will be made when developing the television treatment.

Often, the writer's perception of the communication climate has an impact on the relative emphasis given to the subject matter. For instance, normally, a program introducing a new product to a field sales force will be greeted as a positive communication. However, if research reveals that morale is down due to recent cutbacks in sales personnel and there's been a rash of unsuccessful new product introductions, you may face a negative communication environment. The already overburdened sales force views the new product introduction as another negative. In that event, your critical content focus may need to be placed on topics such as techniques to maximize time and territory management, the competitive viability of the product or the long-term potential of the product and its role in returning the company to a level of profitability that supports an expanded sales force.

In short, get the main points of the video presentation down on paper in a logical sequence. In so doing, both writer and client have an opportunity to focus strictly on content. With a content outline, missing points or extraneous material can be more easily identified. Shifts in emphasis on significant points can also be worked out. And it's all accomplished without the intrusion of stylistic concerns.

SUMMARY

Taken all together, these three elements of the action plan—the audience profile, the statement of objectives and the content outline—give the client a comprehensive report on your research findings. If there are problems or misconceptions, they can be ironed out before script material is generated. And, with these items down on paper, the writer is now prepared to begin tackling the video presentation itself.

5

Visualizing the Program:
The Treatment

To this point, the writer has done a significant amount of work in understanding and delineating the client's communication or training goals. A lot of writing has taken place, giving shape to amorphous research findings and providing feedback to the client. But nothing has yet been said to describe the actual sights and sounds that will flicker across the TV screen. Now comes a significant turning point in the life of any project —the transition from research and organization to conceptual work. The creative concept for a TV script represents the underlying rationale for the entire narrative and visual structure of a program. It's akin to what Henry James called "the germ" for a story or novel.

Creative concepts that spring logically from a thorough consideration of the program's goals and audience pave the way for successful television productions—programming that fulfills stated objectives. A creative concept that is on target will result in good television even in the face of budgetary, production and time limitations. On the other hand, no amount of cosmetic production value will compensate for a presentation based on a bankrupt creative concept. Spend $100,000 or more producing a two-dollar concept and you still end up with a two-dollar concept!

That's why the writer's most significant contribution takes place at this stage in the life of a project, that moment when content begins to take shape as a television viewing experience. Until a specific creative direction is established, the possibilities and potential of a project are infinite. Once writer, client and producer/director agree upon a concept, however, the form and style of the viewing experience are established.

THE TREATMENT

The treatment is the tool the writer uses to communicate his or her vision of the ultimate viewing experience. The treatment is a narrative description of the program in prose form. It does not look like a script, nor does it function like a script. Where a script is a production tool, a treatment is a tool for communicating and discussing the creative concept for a program. It helps the client and others visualize pictorial and narrative elements in nontechnical language. This is important because many nonbroadcast clients suffer from "shooting-script illiteracy."

In order to describe a program not yet produced, however, the writer must first have a "pre-vision" of the finished program, an internal visualization that parallels the ultimate viewing experience. The writer, then, is the first to "see" and "hear" content unfolding just as a viewer would. In effect, the treatment is the writer's notes of what he is "seeing" and "hearing." This does not mean the writer hears every word of narration or sees each visual in the mind's eye. That's overkill. Instead, the writer focuses on major program elements: the opening, key scenes and transitions.

What narrative device will be used to convey verbal information? A series of interviews? A narrator? Or perhaps a dramatization? The treatment should also suggest the visual material that will convey information. Is it documentary footage of a medical procedure? Animation? Or is there a studio setting that contains graphic display areas and props? What overall tone and style does the writer envision? Humor? Documentary reality? Strong dramatic action? Or a straightforward presentation of factual material? Other considerations include the role that music or special video and sound effects might play.

The "pre-vision" should contain enough detail to communicate all major points in the content outline. Not until the concept is complete enough to generate a shooting script is the writer ready to commit his or her vision to paper as a television treatment.

STIMULATING A VISION: USE OF PROGRAM FORMATS

Sometimes the shape and form of a program literally spring full-blown into the writer's consciousness, as though the program has been incubating in the subconscious through the entire research period. Then, when it's time to make the transition to a creative concept, the vision comes quite spontaneously. But that type of creative solution is usually a gift. The most panic-inducing feeling, by far, is to lean back, close your eyes—and come up empty. Nothing. When the subconscious "well" runs dry, the conscious mind tends to choke. What to do in such moments of trauma? Despite the uniqueness of every television presentation, under the surface you will find only a handful of well-worn formats—generic methods of presenting materials, which are worked and reworked to accommodate varying content.

A format is simply a method of presenting information through the television medium and therefore is distinct from both content and style. Content can be dealt with in any format the writer wishes, although generally some will be more appropriate than others. Style is the point of view the writer takes toward both material and format.

When creative concepts fail to come, it's helpful to visualize your material in one or more of these generic formats. Some will appear utterly ludicrous, and you can dismiss that type of program format as inappropriate. Other formats will hold potential yet may not strike you as ideal. Whenever a format holds promise, focus on those content points that it seems to suit best. It's not unusual for programs to contain a carefully balanced mix of several program formats, each designed to carry a specific portion of the message.

The following sections describe five generic program formats that are frequently employed in organizational, medical and educational programming. The writer should be familiar with the advantages and disadvantages of each.

The Talking Head

The talking head is the easiest format to visualize. Imagine a speaker, put words in his or her mouth and you have a talking head. Over the years the talking head format has taken lots of abuse from writers, producers, directors—and audiences. Some of that abuse is rightfully deserved; some not.

On the negative side, the talking head makes minimal use of the medium's strong suit—the capability to *show* while telling. As one corporate communicator put it: "Why not send me an audio tape and a photograph?" Obviously, the talking head lives on because, in many communications, *who* delivers the content is as important as what is said. A presidential address is the ultimate example. When the message comes from the chairman of the board, the chancellor of the university or the physician who pioneered a new surgical technique, what is said carries the added weight of authority and credibility.

Unfortunately, executives and experts who are called upon to deliver a talking head message rarely have sufficient time to prepare and rehearse. Lack of experience leads to lack of confidence, nervousness and stage fright. In addition, most nonprofessionals have a difficult time reading teleprompters. Eye contact wanders; vocal inflection lacks pace and variety. And going the extemporaneous route usually doesn't work either.

Executive personalities are apt to fall victim to the one take syndrome. "That's as good as it's going to get," they snarl at directors. Thus, ironically, the two traits that should surface in a talking head presentation —sincerity and believability—are often lacking.

Nevertheless, there are times when the talking head is a necessary program element. When words you hear in a "pre-vision" belong only in the mouth of the chairman, the president or an acknowledged expert, then perhaps the talking head is justified. In that case, brevity is the operative word for writers (or ghost writers). Get direct input from the person who's going before the cameras. Talking head remarks should be written in the style of the speaker—not the writer. (For more on preparing executives to appear on television, consult *The Executive's Guide to TV and Radio Appearances*.[1])

As a pure format, the talking head should be used judiciously, never running more than three to five minutes. (Think about it; five minutes is a long time to watch the same visual image.) Limit content to those things that only the president or an authority can say. There are better, more visual formats for other content points. Though relatively inexpensive to produce, the talking head is not an economical use of the medium because it is audio-reliant and fails to capitalize on the potent visual capacity of television.

The Talking Head with Props

Give a talking head props to work with, and greater visual content results. A classic example of this format is Julia Child's cooking programs: an enthusiastic, animated talking head demonstrating the fine points of soufflés for a television viewing audience. This format is ideal for many corporate, educational and medical subjects—particularly programming with certain training objectives. The props can, literally, be anything: a real object such as a computer terminal or artwork such as diagrams of the cardiovascular system. It could be a chroma-key (see Glossary) screen used for electronic display of slides or film. Set pieces can be designed to convey visual information and serve as props.

Don't confine yourself to studio-bound productions. A narrator strolling through a manufacturing plant and pointing out stages in an assembly line or touring the facilities of a medical center is simply using a real-life prop to illustrate content. The camera's ability to isolate details on

---

[1]Michael Bland, *The Executive's Guide to TV and Radio Appearances* (White Plains, NY: Knowledge Industry Publications, Inc., 1980).

props through close-ups enables the viewing audience to see what the talking head is describing.

There are, however, inherent dangers in this format. If the props used are unsuited to the horizontal aspect ratio of the TV screen or to the resolution requirements of an electronic picture, visual content will suffer. Julia Child's television kitchen was laid out for optimum camera angles as well as the chef's convenience. For example, the set included a special mirror for looking down onto the range. Another problem also results when the content or sequence of events is not structured for television time. Again, consider how Julia Child chops, mixes, bakes or otherwise prepares stages of a recipe in advance to condense screen time. Television screen time is more concentrated than real time, and the writer must make optimum use of screen time.

Visuals and Voices

With visuals and voices the narrator is heard but not seen. A sequence of visuals fills the screen while narration comments on the action. The visual material may be quite varied: product footage, animation, slides or photographs, artwork, charts, symbols and other graphics—literally almost anything the eye can see and a camera can shoot. And such visual elements can be juxtaposed and intermixed through a variety of video effects and transitions. Sometimes, the visual material may already exist in the form of stock film footage or historical photographs. In those cases, the writer must develop narrative sequences to match. Ideally, however, the writer can start from scratch with the opportunity to create the entire pictorial and narrative experience in the mind's eye.

The writer's goal is to structure sequences where the combined effect of picture and sound equals more than the sum of its parts. This synergistic use of pictures and sound makes the most of the informational capacity of television—an audio-visual medium. Although we call this "Visuals and Voices," don't overlook "Visuals and Music," or "Visuals and Sound Effects." The combination of music and pictures is potent for establishing the mood of the piece or for allowing viewers time to ponder what's been said or to concentrate fully on the visual imagery. "Visuals and Music" is also a good transitional technique.

The visuals and voices format also offers tremendous flexibility for dealing with time and space. It's possible to leap from London to Manila to Los Angeles in a 10-second sequence. Or it's equally possible to draw parallels between Henry Ford's first assembly line and high tech electronically controlled assembly lines of the 1980s in another 10 seconds.

It is also a demanding format. Visual information must be sufficiently varied and move from image to image and scene to scene with sufficient pacing to sustain interest. At the same time, stylistic integrity is necessary to avoid a haphazard potpourri effect. Motion within the frame and/or changes in perspective or visual content must be frequent to keep the presentation from becoming static. From a pure media standpoint, for instance, there's little reason to present a sequence of full-frame slides and narration on television. That communication could easily be accomplished with a synchronized sound-and-slide presentation. If, however, slide content is enhanced by camera moves or titles or special effects, then use of the television medium may be justified.

Another consideration: although a writer may envision a flood of images, sooner or later practical production realities of shooting or gathering that footage within time and budgetary restraints must be faced.

One final point on visuals and voices. Because the narrator goes unseen, this format tends toward the impersonal. Personal messages, subjects that focus on human interactions or topics where expert analysis is needed do not lend themselves to the impersonal, disembodied voice which characterizes this format.

Interviews

What distinguishes the interview from other formats is that, essentially, it is half-scripted. Interview shows are often referred to as unscripted, but good interviews don't just happen. The interviewer must prepare and script major questions and discussion points. The strength of the interview format is that it allows people to be themselves on camera. Interviews convey personality (for better or worse) as well as content. The subject's reaction to a question, the smile that crosses the face during an answer, the pause that telegraphs thought processes—all communicate as much as words themselves by placing the content in the context of character.

This program format contains two distinct sub-categories, the on-camera interview and the off-camera interview. As the name implies, the on-camera interview features the interviewer as an active participant in the program, in the manner of Barbara Walters or David Frost. In the off-camera format, the interviewer is unseen and generally unheard. On-camera interviews usually proceed in linear fashion from beginning to end or at least give the appearance of such continuity. The off-camera interview style results in a less structured, more documentary style, which lends itself to juxtaposing several interviews, in order to organize content topically rather than chronologically.

The most important hurdle for writers is to structure interview sequences so that predetermined content is brought out naturally, even spontaneously, from the interview itself. Scripting answers, however, is asking for trouble. The only reason for interviews in the first place is to allow subjects to choose their own words, to be themselves. Interview content should be prepared in advance but never go so far as to put words in the subject's mouth. We'll discuss interviews more fully in Chapter 9.

Dramatizations

On the surface, dramatizations would appear to have much in common with talking head and interview formats—people talking to one another. The format, however, requires several special skills, and many otherwise good nonbroadcast writers have difficulty with the demands of dramatic action.

Dramatizations are most useful when subject matter focuses on the dynamics of interpersonal relationships: selling techniques, employment interviewing, counselling and other situations that emphasize human interaction. The strength of the dramatization is that it can focus on predictable behaviors. Quite frequently, dramatizations are structured as models for specific situations: how to handle customer complaints; how to conduct performance appraisals; how to overcome objections from prospective buyers. Dramatizations can also demonstrate the consequences of poor interpersonal communications. And this format is a good way to build audience interest or emphathy.

From the writer's viewpoint, two critical skills are needed to construct dramatizations. First, drama involves characters in conflict. This doesn't mean all dramatizations contain the melodramatic overtones of a soap opera. For dramatic human interaction, however, two or more characters must be motivated by objectives that are at cross-purposes in a given situation. Second, drama requires scripted conversation—not narration. Playwrights and screenwriters are known for having "good ears." The nonbroadcast writer who ventures into dramatizations must also develop an ear for dialog. Chapter 10 covers the subject in detail.

Mixing Apples & Oranges

An advertising friend's retort to the old adage "You can't mix apples and oranges," has always stuck in my mind. "Sure you can. It's done every day," he'd say. "It's called a fruit salad." Just like apples and oranges, these five basic formats can be mixed, matched and combined in infinite variety to fit the content and goals of any given communication. In fact, most subjects don't fall neatly into a single, uniform format unless they are very short, five minutes or less in length. More frequently the content of corporate, medical or educational television programming is too complex and varied to fit categorically into a single format, and a typical script involves mixing several formats, as shown in Figure 5.1.

Figure 5.1: Examples of Mixed Script Formats

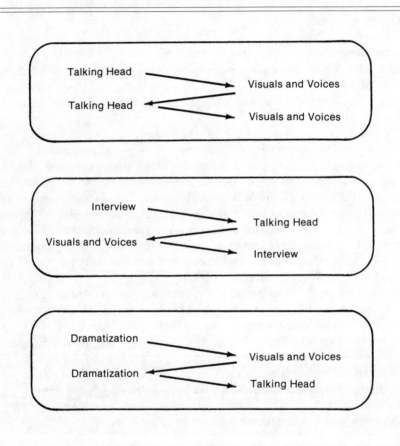

A multitude of combinations is possible. The important point to keep in mind is that the writer's "pre-vision' should be grounded in content, audience and objectives. Allow the material to dictate form. This leads to a format (or combination of formats) that is functional and appropriate.

WRITING THE TREATMENT

When formats are combined, each format should be intended to cover a discrete portion of overall content. What begins to emerge is a breakdown of the action according to scenes. Each scene is a building block within the "chronological sequence of events describing sounds, pictures and ideas." When the writer can encompass all content in a series of scenes, it's time to write the television treatment.

The treatment communicates to the client and director the sights and sounds imagined in the "pre-vision." Although each writer develops his or her own style and shorthand for treatments, most follow these general guidelines:

- Develop the treatment chronologically. Begin with the opening of the program and proceed through major scenes to the conclusion. Describe the format you envision for each scene.

- Describe both sights and sounds. The treatment must convey a sense of the narrative and visual style of the program.

- Describe the cast of characters or participants. Indicate whether they appear on or off camera, whether they are delivering prepared text or responding to interview questions.

- Indicate major transitions—how you plan to proceed from one scene to the next.

To illustrate these guidelines, three annotated excerpts from treatments prepared for informational programs are included at the end of this chapter. The excerpts depict a variety of formats and visual/narrative styles and techniques. Numbers in parentheses in the text correspond to comments, which follow each excerpt and point out how the writer follows the basic guidelines for writing treatments. You should be able to visualize a television viewing experience from each excerpt—not in its entirety but the overall sense.

THE COMPLETE ACTION PLAN

The complete action plan, including an audience profile, objectives, a content outline and a television treatment, marks the end of the research and conceptual phase of a project. Once the client and producer/director approve the action plan, the writer turns to the detailed work of constructing a comprehensive shooting script.

The importance of this preliminary work cannot be overemphasized. Although some things will evolve and change on the road to a final shooting script, the essentials of form and style are established through the television treatment. Therefore it's essential for everyone involved (especially the writer) to recognize the significance of this stage. Those people with the most at stake in the project have now agreed to a specific course of action. To make changes after this point almost always proves counterproductive and generally results in a loss of momentum, production delays, perhaps even unbudgeted expenses. If a decision maker or the writer has reservations or doubts about the direction the project is taking, now is the time to pull back and regroup. If it means returning to the drawing board and developing an entirely new approach, so be it.

Generally, however, thoroughness and good conceptual work up to this point result in an approach that is greeted enthusiastically by everyone involved. In the majority of cases, the writer can now turn to the task of fashioning a shooting script with the confidence that results from a clear focus on where the project is headed and how it will get there.

Scenes from "Why Not Craig Cunningham?" (See Treatment 3.) The production dramatized principles of evaluating disabled job applicants through the story of Craig Cunningham, a blind candidate, who is seen in a job interview (top) and at home with his wife (bottom). Courtesy AT&T.

TREATMENT 1:
CONSUMER CENTER VIDEO PRESENTATION*

We fade up on the entrance to the Consumer Center. **(1)** The shot features the general store display, **(2)** populated by characters in period costume. **(2)** The storekeeper **(3)** banters with a woman **(3)** and her two young children. **(3)** The woman is "stocking her larder" for the month (the kids have only penny candy on their minds). **(3)** The talk is of the weather, crops and "when the new school marm's due to arrive." **(4)**

As the woman runs down her shopping list, she asks to look at a "box of that new Post Cereal." She peruses the package, then asks the storekeeper about its nutritional value or wholesomeness...at that moment the dramatic action freezes, forming a tableau. **(5)** The Narrator (possibly a woman) enters frame and addresses the camera.

"Consumers have always had questions about the products we make. As long ago as 1925, two home economists were hired by the company to form an educational department and provide nutrition information about Post cereals and Postum beverages. Today, that department is known as the General Foods Consumer Center." **(6)**

On this last line, the camera pans to the wall with contemporary "Consumer Center" graphics. **(7)** Music and actuality audio **(8)** punctuate a fast-paced montage of Consumer Center activities: pies going into a test kitchen oven; a photographer lighting a main dish still life; a high-speed word processing machine banging out a consumer response letter; a group of division and agency people participating in an intense taste-testing.

Interwoven with these glimpses of Consumer Center activities is additional voice-over copy. The Narrator reinforces the pictorial impression that the Consumer Center involves many diverse activities. "All these activities mirror General Foods' responsiveness to consumer needs and concerns." **(9)**

The narration establishes that in this program "we'll see and hear how each area of the Consumer Center advocates the interests of the consumer in all aspects of General Foods' business."

This opening montage comes to an end with the program title—then fades momentarily to black.

Commentary

(1) In contrast to content outlines (which are structured in topical outline

---

*From a proposal by William Van Nostran for a General Foods consumer education project.

fashion), the treatment describes the program according to the chronological sequence of events that will take place on the screen.

(2) The research agenda obviously included a site survey of the Consumer Center. Research notes make reference to a nineteenth-century general store display as an ideal spot for location shooting and an opening historical vignette.

(3) The cast of characters is fully identified. Stage business for "two young children" is sketchy in the treatment. That business will, more than likely, be described in greater detail in the shooting script. For a treatment, simply paint mental pictures in bold, vivid strokes.

(4) Quotes telegraph the style of the dialog,which will ultimately be scripted verbatim.

(5) The writer sets up the Narrator's entrance by calling for the dramatic action to freeze.

(6) More detailed copy indicates the writer's vision of narrative style.

(7) An important visual transition is described in terms of action that will be seen on the screen. (Again, it's apparent that the writer's research has included site surveys and that accurate notes were taken on the relationship between various locales.)

(8) Also part of the writer's concept is the use of music and actuality audio (speech and sound effects captured during location shooting; this lends authenticity and should not be scripted in advance).

(9) Notice that a treatment is merely a distillation of content. Specifics for this segment can be cross-referenced to the content outline. Don't belabor details in the treatment.

TREATMENT 2:
EXTRA CARE TEAM COMMUNICATION*

Introduce the Product: Single Patient Dialysis System (1)

Dip to black, then up again on footage of a dialysis patient hooking up to Extracorporeal's single patient dialysis instrument in a home environment. Mix actuality audio with interview comments of patient describing his/her condition, history and dialysis regimen. During actuality moments, main program titles appear over action.

The Tampa Story

A Productivity Case Study:
Quality Circles

The patient's final interview comment describes what the dialysis machine means in terms of coping with this condition. The off-camera narration picks up on the patient's final comment: "The dialysis instrument which means so much to (*patient's name*) was made right here."

Establish Extracorporeal Plant (1)

Dissolve through to plant activity as narrator makes transition. Supers identify locale: (2)

Extracorporeal Medical Specialities, Inc.
Tampa, Florida

The narrator provides a brief statistical profile of the facility in terms of size, number of employees, product line, etc. The camera appears to rove through the plant, cinema verité style, capturing daily work scenes. (3) Whenever appropriate, hard data is supered to augment the narrator's profile.

At one point, we peer into a meeting room where an Extra Care Team session is in progress. As the camera moves inside, the narrator explains that we're "watching a Quality Circle in action. This is what brought us to Extracorporeal in Tampa. We wanted to see how employees go about identifying and solving work-related problems through Quality Circles.

---

* From a proposal by William Van Nostran for a Johnson & Johnson project, "The Extra Care Story: A Quality Circle Case Study."

And just what impact has this Quality Circle concept had on productivity and quality at this plant? We began by asking what led Extracorporeal to adopt the Quality Circle concept in the first place." (4)

Background (1)

The scene shifts to the general manager's area, where we see Jim Kilgore interacting with office staff members. Narration sets the stage for interview comments: "Jim Kilgore describes the situation at Extracorporeal when he became the plant's new General Manager in 1978..."

Cut to interview footage of Kilgore (5) describing "inherited" problems: order backlogs, rework, absenteeism, etc. The cumulative effect of this productivity shortfall was being felt in the bottom line.

Narrator introduces Ben Robling, Quality Control Manager. In interview footage, he describes his first exposures to the Quality Circle concept. (5) Intercut Robling comments with the Kilgore interview as they recount the initial factors and concerns that influenced their decision to start a Quality Circle. They refer to the role of an outside consultant, and we cut to interview footage of Dr. Richard Hess, (5) explaining the involvement of his firm, Productivity Development Systems. Rhythmic intercutting among Kilgore, Robling and Hess as they address major considerations and prerequisite training needed for Quality Circle start-up.

Commentary

(1) The writer envisions program content as major program segments, or scenes, each with a single purpose.

(2) Transitions from scene to scene are indicated, as well as "supers" or titles that appear on-screen to identify locale.

(3) The writer is establishing a visual style through this description of camera work.

(4) Likewise, short segments of narrative copy provide a feel for how the writer intends to treat the narration.

(5) The treatment includes several interview segments. Here, the writer identifies who is to appear on camera and the content which interview questions will elicit. (This treatment suggests the writer's research agenda included interviews with these individuals.)

TREATMENT 3:
EEO POLICY — THE HANDICAPPED INTERVIEW*

We fade up on an office scene and meet Donna Walker, a black female personnel interviewer. She's talking with Lou Cushner, a middle level manager. Lou has just gone through applications of several "best qualified" candidates for a position he's trying to fill. We pick up the dialog at the point where Donna challenges Lou, (1) asking why he doesn't want to see Craig Cunningham—a candidate Donna thinks is well qualified.

Lou responds forthrightly: "Donna, now I know you look at these things from a different perspective—but you can't expect me to seriously consider a blind person for this job." (2)

Donna counters: "I'm asking you to consider Craig Cunningham—who happens to be qualified, capable and, yes, blind." (2)

Lou continues, however, down the predictable path of objections that spring from typical core beliefs. (3) Because of his handicap, Lou assumes Craig couldn't possibly carry a full share of the workload. Training and day-to-day supervision would prove too time-consuming. There's likely to be resentment from the rest of the staff.

After letting Lou give expression to his full complement of stereotypes and uninformed core beliefs, Donna takes a different tack: "Let's approach it from another angle. You tell me again the basic duties that a systems analyst is supposed to perform."

Lou ticks off the duties and requirements of the job. As Lou catalogs job requirements, Donna assures him she feels confident Craig meets those specific requirements. "I don't think you've told me anything that would disqualify Craig to this point. I recall his interview quite well..."

At this point, we use a "flashback" technique and go back in time to Donna's initial interview with Craig. (4) Through the interview, we learn about Craig's background and experience—the fact that he has a dual major in business administration and marketing, that he was a lieutenant in the army and worked with outside suppliers and contractors in procurement. Since becoming blind shortly after discharge, however, his "career has taken a backseat." Craig explains that his adjustment to blindness has been time-consuming and, at times, frustrating. He's now adept at braille, however, and feels more confident about his mobility with the cane. For almost a year now, Craig has worked part time doing telephone contact work. He freely admits, though, that because of his college training and army experience in management, he "wants a career —not just a job."

---

*From a proposal by William Van Nostran for an AT&T project, "Why Not Craig Cunningham?"

At an appropriate moment, we return to Donna and Lou—as though Donna has just recapped that portion of the interview for Lou. **(4)** Although apparently willing to give Craig more serious consideration, Lou is still in the "doubting Thomas" mode. "Well...granted, he might be qualified. But you can't tell me his handicap's not going to get in the way. I mean, for one thing—we get tons of raw data in real time from CRT terminals. Sure, supervisors don't have to *operate* those terminals—but they all get outputs from them constantly..." **(2)**

(Later in this treatment, new characters, scenes and styles are introduced.)

The next major program segment shows Craig in his home environment—the evening prior to his job tour interview. Rather than striving for the continuity of an entire evening, however, this segment will consist of brief, pithy moments between Craig and his wife, Maureen. A revue style "black out" technique will be used to punctuate each vignette. **(5)** Taken all together, these vignettes will illuminate Craig's personality, strong desire to excel, ability to cope despite his disability and doubts about finding a managerial position.

Another dramatic technique in this segment will be the use of voice-over bridges from the point of view of Maureen. **(6)** This is an expeditious way to convey information relating to Craig's convalescence. It also offers a means for describing Craig's frustration and repeated job rejections without becoming melodramatic.

The vignettes themselves, low-key in style and tone, **(5)** depict a normal relationship between a young couple who have adjusted to the changes a disability brings to their lives. We listen in, for example, on after supper banter as Craig and Maureen do the dishes. Maureen washes—Craig dries and stacks.

Commentary

(1) This is a dramatization. Notice how the writer establishes conflict in the very first paragraph.

(2) Dialog provides insight into the conversation that will take place between Lou and Donna.

(3) Detailed content can likely be found in a content outline under the heading "Core Beliefs about the Handicapped."

(4) Flashback transitions describe the writer's intent to deal with time in fluid, yet structured, transitional sequences. This time shift mode is established early on.

(5) Notice again how the writer is preoccupied with style and narrative technique in the treatment—not with detailed content.

(6) Even in this essentially dramatic piece, the writer suggests the use of a narrator. In this case, the narrator will be a character from the dramatic vignettes. Narration will need to be written "in character"—appropriate dialog and thoughts for Maureen.

6

Structuring the Script

There are good reasons for preparing your manuscripts in a standard video or film format. The most obvious is that a shooting script, as the name implies, functions as a blueprint that the production team must be able to follow in constructing the ultimate viewing experience. On the most superficial level, the mechanics of setting up and following shooting script formats appear to have more to do with typing than creative writing. But if you gloss over this chapter, dog-earing it for your secretary or typist to read, you're missing the point of writing for television.

The format of a shooting script is a means of structuring that "chronological sequence of events describing sounds, pictures and ideas" in written form. Stripped of content (the ideas), television is a three-dimensional medium consisting of sights and sounds existing in time. To construct a functional shooting script from the skeletal structure of the treatment, the writer labors in painstaking detail, setting down on paper a sequence of visual and auditory cues that unfold second by second, minute by minute. Successful writers develop a keen sense of sculpting time through words on paper with full knowledge that the words themselves are not as important as the events they describe.

THE TELEVISION CONTINUUM

When you watch television, you're really looking at a continuous evolution of spatial relationships between camera and subject. Concurrently, you hear a continuous mix of music, voices, sound effects or, occasionally, total silence. Time binds the two together. To describe those spatial relationships and auditory events, the writer uses a special vocabulary. Some terms describe the spatial relationship between camera and subject: long shot (LS), medium shot (MS), close-up (CU), and extreme close-up (ECU). (Figure 6.1 illustrates each.) Other terms define the movement of the camera in relation to the subject: pan left or right; zoom in or out; dolly in or truck right. (See Glossary for definitions.) Even

Figure 6.1: Camera Shots

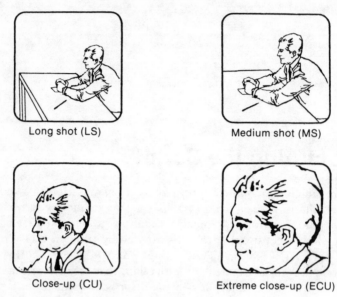

Long shot (LS)   Medium shot (MS)

Close-up (CU)   Extreme close-up (ECU)

within a static shot, where the camera remains completely fixed, the writer often describes an evolving spatial relationship:

MS—On female
narrator in park
setting. Background
action consists of
teenage boys tossing
football or frisbee.

These terms are the basic vocabulary of television or, for that matter, film. The terminology is a functional "shorthand." In a similar manner, the writer also indicates words to be spoken to accompany visuals; music to establish mood, time or locale; sound effects to punctuate on-screen action. Space and sound, then, are two of television's three dimensions that the writer shapes.

But how is the medium's third dimension, time, expressed on paper? Remember, scripts are rendered obsolete by finished television programs. Words on paper are always translated into *space and sound in time*. Thus, a half-hour program always requires 30 minutes to watch. (Random access programming is one new, exciting exception.) The writer's use of time is known as "pacing." In most nonbroadcast scripts, time is generally measured by the duration of audio events. A segment of narration takes 10 seconds to read; a musical interlude lasts 45 seconds; a sound effect occurs for three seconds. (You might even script 11 seconds of silence to achieve a specific effect.)

THE SPLIT-PAGE FORMAT

The television writer is constantly "orchestrating" three raw materials. A script shows simultaneously

spatial events, which describe the visual content of specific shots,	and	auditory information, which includes narrative copy, music, sound effects.

If we orchestrate visual and auditory elements side by side as shown above, we have the classic split-page format of the television shooting script:

VIDEO	AUDIO
Visual events are described on the *left* of the page, under the general heading of "Video."	NARRATION, DIALOG, INTERVIEW COMMENTS, MUSIC, SOUND EFFECTS AND THE LIKE APPEAR ON THE *RIGHT* SIDE OF THE PAGE UNDER THE HEADING "AUDIO."

Time, the third element, is the glue that binds the two events together. But why all the emphasis on time, instead of on what the viewer actually sees and hears? In the nonbroadcast field, subject matter is highly specialized. Frequently, writers place too little emphasis on the *ultimate viewing experience.* In dealing with large blocks of informational copy, the writer must recognize how the duration of audio events on the right side of the page establishes the pacing of the viewing experience. One full page of narration, typed double-spaced on the right side of the page, equals about 60 seconds of screen time. For every page of narration, the viewer must also be *seeing* something for 60 seconds!

The left side of the page, the visual portion of the program, must be synchronized to the auditory cues on the right side of the page. For example, look at this excerpt from an American Express project:[1]

---

[1]From "TRIPS: Your Selling and Servicing Partner," written by Allen Neil, directed by James G. Libby, produced by Video Marketing Group for American Express Travel Services Division. Used by permission.

VIDEO	AUDIO
LS—Wide angle view of model office. Narrator moves towards TRIPS terminal.	**NARRATOR**: OUR NEW TRAVEL SERVICE OFFICE—MODERN, COMFORTABLE, SPACIOUS. THE OFFICE ITSELF SAYS "PRESTIGE, INTEGRITY, SECURITY AND SERVICE."
ZOOM in to MS of Narrator and terminal.	THIS IS THE TRIPS TERMINAL, AND AS YOU CAN SEE, IT'S RIGHT AT HOME IN OUR NEW ENVIRONMENT.
CU—On Narrator.	BUT WHAT IS TRIPS? TRIPS IS A MULTI-ACCESS RETAIL RESERVATIONS, ACCOUNTING AND COMMUNICATIONS SYSTEM. . . AND TO CALL IT REVOLUTIONARY IS AN UNDERSTATEMENT. THE TRIPS COMPUTER SYSTEM PUTS THE WHOLE WORLD OF TRAVEL INFORMATION *LITERALLY* AT YOUR FINGERTIPS.
ECU—Of hands on terminal keyboard.	IT'S AS SIMPLE AS A TYPEWRITER. . . AND AS NEW AS TOMORROW.
ECU—On CRT screen displaying information.	IT'S A NEW WAY OF HANDLING INFORMATION. . .
Info on CRT screen changes rapidly two or three times. Screen now shows the artwork graphic of globe with animated network.	ALL KINDS OF INFORMATION. IT'S A NEW METHOD TO ENHANCE OUR WORLD-WIDE DISTRIBUTION NETWORK. . .OUR WHOLE MARKETING EFFORT.
MS—On Narrator and terminal.	IT'S A NEW TECHNIQUE TO EXPAND OUR CUSTOMER SERVICE CAPABILITIES. TRIPS MAKES AVAILABLE, FOR THE FIRST TIME ANYWHERE, *ALL* OF OUR TRAVEL RESOURCES

ON A MULTI-ACCESS TERMINAL:

Cut to MS on jet liner taking off.	......AIRLINES......
Cut to MS on exterior of famous hotel.	......HOTELS......
Cut to MS of tour bus or group tour.	......TOURS......
Cut to MS of car rental area in airport terminal.	......CAR RENTALS......
ECU—On terminal with display.	......OTHER TRS SYSTEMS......
MS—On Narrator by terminal.	EVERYTHING—RIGHT HERE ON THIS ONE SCREEN.

Using a fundamental progression of long shot to medium shot to close-up, this writer first establishes the scene with a wide angle view, then calls for close-ups to illustrate specific copy points in greater detail. In this sequence of about 90 seconds, the writer calls for 12 different shots. Furthermore, there's an integral relationship between shooting instructions on the left and the narrator's copy on the right. For instance, the writer clearly wants to see a "CU of hands on keyboard" at the precise moment when the narrator says: "It's as simple as a typewriter." Or, when the narrator states "all kinds of information," the writer calls for a "quick change" in the "info on the CRT screen."

This format is known as a shooting script because it provides sufficient detail for a production crew to execute the program from written instructions describing what will happen on the screen moment by moment. This shooting script format cements the synchronization between visual and auditory events occuring in time.

Cues for visual events need not be limited to words. In this script excerpt, specific visual elements are tied to music cues.[2]

---

[2]From "Plain Talk About Our Trademarks," written by William Van Nostran, produced and directed by William J. Benham for AT&T Corporate Communication TV Center. Used by permission.

VIDEO	AUDIO
MS—On Narrator and screen.	**NARRATOR**: . . .NOTICE THAT THE DISPLAY LINE CONSISTS OF TWO ELEMENTS: FIRST, THERE'S THE BELL SYMBOL...
Animated Bell Symbol "floats" into position in screen area.	**MUSIC**: (Short phrase to identify the Bell Symbol. This phrase becomes synonymous with the appearance of the symbol.)
	NARRATOR: THEN, THERE'S A DISTINCTIVE LOGOTYPE.
Animated logotype "floats" into position.	**MUSIC**: (Short phrase to identify the logotype element. Combined with previous musical phrase, it should convey a sense of completion.)

The left and right sides of the page are a unified entity in the above examples. This event-driven writing style distinguishes professional scriptwriters from the amateurs. Whenever the left side of the page lacks shot by shot detailed descriptions of spatial relationships, it's a dead giveaway that the writer focused on developing narrative copy at the expense of visualization. This makes for neither good pictures nor good narration.

Too many nonbroadcast television scripts are created by writing the right side first, then returning to fill in left side visuals as an afterthought. As a result narrative copy tends to be wordy and lengthy, too much like a speech. And, since the writer is stressing only verbal continuity, visual continuity goes by the boards. The skilled television writer searches for the potential synergism between pictures and sound. In fact, much of the visualization springs from the treatment. The script simply expands the details of the original "visions" so that the total viewing experience becomes greater than the sum of its parts. Effective visualization generally reduces the need for explanatory verbalization.

STRUCTURAL BUILDING BLOCKS

Ideally, then, each page of a shooting script is composed shot by shot— so the writer describes the visual image or action on the left side of the page and the copy or other auditory material on the right side. The television writer must learn to see pictures and hear words at the same time. And the shot, with its accompanying text, music or sound, becomes the basic building block of the television writer.

As a general rule of thumb, you should call for new visual information at least every 15 seconds. Relate that to the time equation of the split-page shooting script format, and it works out to at least four shots per page, sometimes many more. Rarely should there be any fewer. This isn't to say your shots will be evenly distributed, one every quarter page. The frequency and duration of a shot depends on many factors: the visual content of the shot, the action that takes place within the frame, movement of camera in relation to the subject. Obviously, more complex, visually dense compositions call for more screen time than a static shot that contains minimal visual detail. (In Chapter 7, we'll analyze visualization as a separate entity. For now, we're focusing on the correlation between sight and sound.)

The general mood, tone and energy of a segment also influence the pacing of visual shots. A series of quick cut shots, in which the viewer is unlikely to absorb the complete details, is more suitable to an up-tempo program segment where the writer strives to create an energetic, fast-paced mood. A series of longer, static shots is more appropriate to the pacing of a segment designed to create an air of tranquility and reflection.

VISUAL TRANSITIONS

Just as a series of individual shots creates a scene, a total program consists of a series of interrelated scenes. Obviously, scene changes occur whenever action moves from one location to another. Additionally, major shifts in subject matter, the introduction of new faces or voices or the passage of time may also correspond to scene changes. Sometimes, scenes are delineated by a significant change in program format—say, moving from an interview segment to a section containing visuals and voices. Scene changes may even be cued by introducing a new style, mood, tone or tempo.

The writer's bridges linking one scene to the next are also written using television production language. Let's look at the terms most frequently used to describe transitions.

Fade to Black/Fade Up

All television programs begin and end in "black." The very first image fades up from a black screen, and the final image fades to black. In addition, a momentary fade to black (sometimes referred to as touching black) then fading in the next scene can also be used as a transitional device to bridge program segments. Generally, this transitional effect is too interruptive to serve as a frequent transition between one scene and another. However, nonbroadcast programming designed for group discussion or other interactions often uses as much as 8 to 10 seconds of black to allow for the mechanics of stopping and restarting playback equipment.

Cut

A cut is nothing more than an instantaneous change between two shots. The final frame of Scene A is followed by the first frame of Scene B. (The term cut originates from motion picture editing, where one piece of film is literally cut and butt-spliced to the preceding shot.) Although a writer may use a cut to go from one scene to the next, it doesn't mean every cut is a transitional device. The simple cut from one camera angle to another, from one image to the next is the normal method of going from shot to shot. A cut between one shot and the next is always implied in a shooting script unless the writer indicates otherwise.

Dissolve

Since the cut is so common, it may not signal shifts in locale, time or content as vividly as the writer might like. The dissolve is an extremely functional way of joining two scenes. In a dissolve, the tail end of Scene A fades out while the first frames of Scene B simultaneously fade in. The two images overlap for a period of time. It's a fluid transition, and since the effect itself requires screen time to occur, it telegraphs to the viewer that a change is taking place.

Wipe

The wipe is sometimes described as a hard-edged dissolve. It looks as though Scene A is being wiped off the screen by the appearance of Scene B. A hard line separates the new scene from the previous scene. The mid-point of a wipe is like a split screen with half of Scene A on one side and half of Scene B on the other. (Like most visual effects, a verbal description sounds more complex than it really is.) A wipe between scenes can move from screen left to screen right, or vice versa. A horizontal wipe moves up or down the screen; a diagonal wipe starts out in one of the four corners of the frame. A series of wipes between relatively short but closely related scenes can be an effective, up-beat way of going from one to the next. Stylistically, the wipe calls attention to itself more than the dissolve. Always be certain the transitional effect is appropriate to the style and tone of the program.

Special Effect Transitions

When a writer feels the need for a still more pronounced stylistic transitional device, a variety of special effect transitions may be written into a script. Here's where a good grasp of editing equipment and techniques helps express visual continuity on the printed page in practical production terminology. Several of these transitional techniques are created by a special effects generator and video switcher and are just more complex versions of a basic wipe. Effects such as a clock wipe, circle wipe, diamond wipe, triangle wipe and the like are variations on a theme using shapes and repeated patterns to achieve distinct looks.

A new post-production editing tool, known as the Quantel or digital effects generator, gives video tape editors unusual flexibility in manipulating the size and perspective of a single image. Using digital effects, transitions such as simulated page turn, flip-flopping pictures, infinity zooms and other types of optical magic can be created within the editing suite.

Custom Transitional Device

Sometimes the writer will even customize a unique transitional device as part of the overall visualization. A custom-tailored transitional effect should, however, be genuinely motivated by content. In the case of the American Express script excerpted earlier, part of the intended message was to dramatize the world-wide application of the new computerized TRavel Information Processing System (TRIPS). In that instance, the writer magically transported the narrator to American Express travel offices around the globe through a specially devised three-dimensional cube which appeared initially as the American Express logo. (See Figure 6.2.) Here's how the transitional effect was described in the shooting script:

VIDEO	AUDIO
MS—On Narrator by terminal.	NARRATOR: . . .TO SEE THE RESULTS OF THAT PLANNING AND DESIGNING, LET'S LOOK AT TRIPS IN ACTION AND SEE ALL THE THINGS IT CAN DO FOR THE CUSTOMER. . .AND FOR US!
On his final word,	OUR FIRST STOP IS OUR PARK

Figure 6.2 For a project on the American Express TRIPS system, the writer suggested a custom transitional device: a cube that reveals upcoming scenes as it rotates. Courtesy American Express Travel Services Division.

the picture
FREEZES and the
camera pulls back to
reveal frozen image
on one face of blue
American Express
cube. The cube begins
to rotate. . .

AVENUE OFFICE IN NEW YORK CITY.

MUSIC: (transitional "tag" theme comes up
to accompany scene change.)

it continues to turn
until the new face,
containing a frozen
image of Narrator
outside Park Avenue
office is full-front and
the preceding scene is
gone. Camera moves
in, losing the box, as
the scene comes alive.

MS—On Narrator.
Follow as he enters
office.

NARRATOR: WHEN AMERICAN EX-
PRESS ENTERED THE TRAVEL BUSI-
NESS BACK IN 1915, PROVIDING
TRAVEL SERVICES AND MAKING
TRAVEL ARRANGEMENTS WAS
RELATIVELY SIMPLE. . .

Such a unique and technically complex transition was justified in this instance because of the importance of the communication. Effect for the sake of effect, however, is invariably self-defeating in nonbroadcast programming. Ninety percent of the time, you will be well served by cuts, dissolves and simple fades. Special effect transitions should be the exception, not the rule. Otherwise, they become unspecial effects.

AUDIO TRANSITIONS

The television writer constructs shooting scripts to show a direct correlation between picture and sound. Thus, the method employed to bridge the audio between one scene and the next is as important as visual transitions. Of course, not all transitions need to be done with trumpets blaring. Often, a simple, slow dissolve with no sound whatsoever suits the writer's stylistic intent ideally. In that case, silence is a functional element within the shooting script, just as white space is functional in a publication.

One straightforward way to bridge the aural transition between two scenes is by cross-fading the two sound tracks. The audio in Scene A goes under as Scene B's audio is brought up. Cross-fading often accompanies a visual dissolve since the two techniques are quite compatible. A related bridging technique, L cutting, brings in the audio from Scene B as the Scene A picture continues for a few seconds. The change in the sound track cues the audience to expect a visual transition just ahead.

Appropriate music and sound effects do much to support, punctuate and add to the effectiveness of visual transitions. The excerpt that follows, from an insurance company historical piece, illustrates how both visual and audio transitions work in tandem.[3]

VIDEO	AUDIO
MS—On artwork of 18th century cargo ship.	**NARRATOR**: THIS EARLY METHOD OF UNDERWRITING ALSO DEMON- STRATES A BASIC PRINCIPLE OF IN- SURANCE—VALID TO THIS DAY; INSURANCE IS A MEANS OF SPREADING RISK.
SUPER: Flashing lightning bolt to sim- ulate storm.	**SOUND EFFX**: (Crack of thunder.)
	NARRATOR: WE'LL LEARN MORE ABOUT HOW THE ART OF UNDERWRITING HAS EVOLVED. BUT FOR NOW, LET'S JUMP FORWARD FROM ENGLAND IN THE 1770s TO NEW YORK CITY IN 1822.
Lose focus on cargo ship. . . DISSOLVE	**MUSIC AND SOUND EFFX**: (Theme from Dvorak's "New World" mixed with sounds of the city—trolley car, carriages, etc.)
and refocus on view of 19th century New York City. Continue with series of shots cut to audio.	**NARRATOR**: IN 1822, LOTS OF THINGS WERE STILL BRAND NEW IN THE "NEW WORLD."

[3]From "Crum and Forster Orientation," written and produced by William Van Nostran, directed by James G. Libby. Copyright Crum & Forster Corporation, 1982. Used by permission.

The effect of the visual transition, which involves a loss of focus, dissolve to another out-of-focus image and a refocus, is heightened by a purposeful use of music and sound effects. Furthermore, the sound effects add a sense of presence to the shots of early New York City.

OTHER PAGE FORMATS

The split-page format has evolved as the standard for professional television scripting, including the nonbroadcast realm. However, for the nonbroadcast field, the split-page format carries certain liabilities. As pointed out in Chapter 1, one of the limited number of shooting script readers is the client, who often has no background in television production. Even such rudimentary abbreviations as LS, MS, CU and ECU can prove bewildering to this reader.

The more secure client will come right out and ask, "Just what does MS mean?" Frequently, however, the client confronted by the left side page jargon gets frustrated and reads only the narrative copy. This can be dangerous, paving the way for a multitude of surprises and misunderstandings once the production crew takes over. It is good practice to present draft scripts in person and offer a verbal overview of setting, action and visual/narrative style. In addition, there are two alternate methods of page formatting, motion picture formats and storyboarding, that should also be part of the nonbroadcast television writer's repertoire. Both can help overcome problems associated with a right-side-only reader.

Motion Picture Format

The motion picture format is the standard within the film industry for features, television drama shot on film, documentary and informational pictures. Although this format still relies upon the use of production terminology, the relationship between picture and sound is expressed differently on the printed page. Below, we've recast the American Express excerpt, seen previously in split-page format, into a motion picture format.

1. INT. WIDE ANGLE SHOT OF TRAVEL OFFICE. NARRATOR ENTERS AND MOVES TOWARD TRIPS TERMINAL.

NARRATOR
(Addressing camera.) Our new Travel
Service Office—modern, comfortable,
spacious. The office itself says "prestige,
integrity, security and service."

2. ZOOM IN TO TWO-SHOT OF NARRATOR AND TERMINAL.

> **NARRATOR**
> This is the TRIPS terminal. And, as you
> can see, it's right at home in our new
> environment.

3. CLOSE-UP ON NARRATOR.

> **NARRATOR**
> But what is TRIPS? TRIPS is a multi-
> access retail reservations, accounting and
> communications system. . .and to call it
> revolutionary is an understatement. The
> TRIPS computer system puts the whole
> world of travel information *literally* at your
> fingertips.

4. EXTREME CLOSE-UP OF HANDS OPERATING KEYBOARD
   TERMINAL.

> **NARRATOR**
> It's as simple as a typewriter. . .and as new
> as tomorrow.

5. EXTREME CLOSE-UP ON CRT SCREEN DISPLAYING
   INFORMATION.

> **NARRATOR**
> It's a new way of handling information. . .

6. INFO ON CRT SCREEN CHANGES RAPIDLY TWO OR
   THREE TIMES.

> **NARRATOR**
> all kinds of information. It's a new method
> to enhance our world-wide distribution net-
> work. . .

7. MEDIUM SHOT ON NARRATOR AND TERMINAL.

> **NARRATOR**
> It's a new technique to expand our customer
> service capabilities. TRIPS makes available,

for the first time anywhere, *all* of our travel
resources on a multi-access terminal:

8. EXT. - CLOSE-UP SHOT OF JET LINER TAKING OFF.

NARRATOR
Airlines. . .

9. EXT. - MEDIUM SHOT OF FAMOUS HOTEL ENTRANCE.

NARRATOR
Hotels. . .

10. EXT. - MEDIUM SHOT OF TOUR BUS OR TOUR GROUP.

NARRATOR
Tours. . .

11. EXT. - MEDIUM SHOT OF CAR RENTAL AREA IN
AIRPORT TERMINAL.

NARRATOR
Car rentals. . .

12. INT. - EXTREME CLOSE-UP ON TERMINAL WITH
DISPLAY.

NARRATOR
Other TRS systems. . .

13. INT. - MEDIUM SHOT OF NARRATOR BY TERMINAL.

NARRATOR
Everything—right here on this one screen.

The distinction between picture and sound in the motion picture format
is delineated by typography and margin settings. Each camera shot is
numbered and below and within each shot, narration, music and sound
effects are described. Changes of setting are indicated with the shot
description—INT. for interior shots, EXT. for exterior shots. This format
does make it more difficult to ignore visuals and read only narrative copy.
However, it is probably no less bewildering to the client with little or no
media background. Both television and motion picture script formats
require visualization skills to go from printed page to pictures in the mind's
eye.

Storyboards

When you wish to be absolutely certain the client's perception of visual imagery is clear, the surest technique is the television storyboard.

Ad agencies storyboard all commercials using the format shown in Figure 6.3. This format is eminently practical for communicating a 30-or even 60-second message to a client. But for programs of 15, 20, 30 minutes or longer, the advertising storyboard does not allow sufficient room for detailed copy. So, most nonbroadcast scripts that are storyboarded use a split-page format with audio instructions on the right as usual. On the left, however, artists' renderings or sketches take the place of verbal TV production instructions. Figure 6.4 shows a segment of the familiar American Express example in storyboard format.

The advantages are quite obvious—visual content is communicated visually rather than verbally. There's a much greater chance that the client, content experts and production crew will all be picturing identical images. The storyboard can illustrate the interplay of words and picture when the visual content is complex or varied or involves unusual sets, props or effects that are difficult to describe verbally.

In fact, the storyboard appears so functional, one might wonder why it's not universally used. Two reasons: some program formats really don't require storyboarding; and most writers can't draw. Let's tackle the latter problem first. To be effective, a storyboard must clearly convey the essence of a shot. My own attempts at storyboarding usually leave the bewildered client asking "What's that supposed to be?" (How do I then tactfully say "That's you?") Of course, there are exceptions to the writers can't draw argument; the writer who's comfortable storyboarding should do so, by all means.

The rest of us, however, must work with an artist. That's when it becomes pertinent to ask: "Does this concept require storyboarding?" In an interview format, for instance, there's little need to storyboard a sequence of talking heads. Or when the visual material is familiar and consists of real life objects, it's sufficient to write "CU—On hands operating keyboard." It doesn't take great imaginative powers to visualize that shot. Also, when dealing with elaborate sets, your artist's time may be better spent doing a large rendering of the set rather than storyboarding each individual shot.

As a basic rule, then, use the split-page format for most projects. It is functional for the production crew and can be understood by most clients with a little explanation. Use of a script format itself communicates to the client that you are, indeed, a professional TV writer. If you feel the storyboard is justified, then use it. But be certain to work closely with an artist who can storyboard quickly and clearly if you write but don't draw.

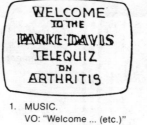

1. MUSIC.
   VO: "Welcome ... (etc.)"

2. BKGD MUSIC.
   VO: (Instructions)

3. BKGD MUSIC.

4. MUSIC FADES.
   VO: "Welcome to Parke-Davis Research Labs. Let's take a minute to talk about rheumatoid arthritis."

5. VO: "Here's a patient with a moderate case of arthritis. The patient has a history of (...) and is now complaining of (...)."

6. VO: "This form of arthritis is quite painful. Is it caused by ...?"

7. VO: (Read four choices).

8. VO: (After pause to allow participant's choice) "The correct answer is C ... (repeat correct answer)."

Figure 6.3 Advertising agencies generally storyboard with copy lines placed under each visual frame. That technique is adapted here for a storyboard used in a proposal to help the client visualize an interactive video disc application for medical conventions. (VO: voice over.) Courtesy O'Hara Company.

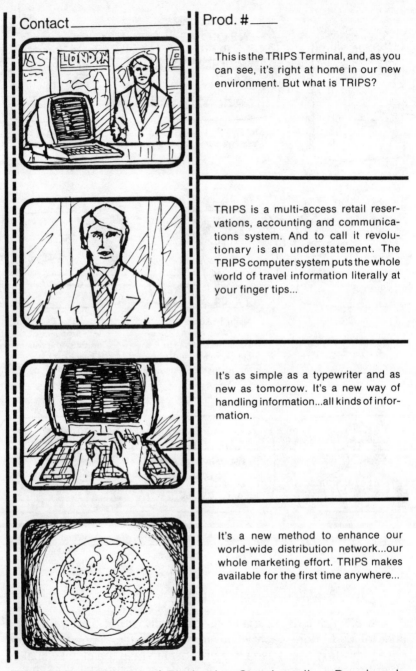

Contact_____   Prod. #____

This is the TRIPS Terminal, and, as you can see, it's right at home in our new environment. But what is TRIPS?

TRIPS is a multi-access retail reservations, accounting and communications system. And to call it revolutionary is an understatement. The TRIPS computer system puts the whole world of travel information literally at your finger tips...

It's as simple as a typewriter and as new as tomorrow. It's a new way of handling information...all kinds of information.

It's a new method to enhance our world-wide distribution network...our whole marketing effort. TRIPS makes available for the first time anywhere...

Figure 6.4: Illustration of Production Storyboarding. Drawings by John Onuschak.

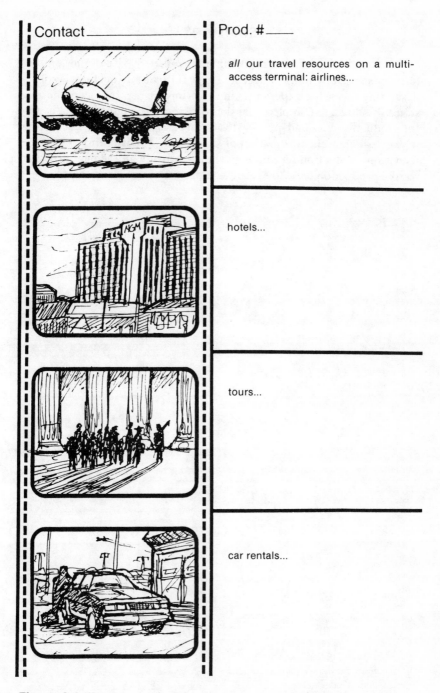

Contact _____   Prod. # ____

all our travel resources on a multi-access terminal: airlines...

hotels...

tours...

car rentals...

Figure 6.4 Illustration of Production Storyboarding (cont.)

SUMMARY

The writer must always think simultaneously in visual and auditory terms. The various industry-accepted page formats are functional tools for describing a viewing experience on the printed page. In fact, a shooting script should be so complete that the writer could turn the project over to the production crew and move on to another assignment. Whatever format is selected, careful coordination of sights and sounds in time and use of television production terminology should provide all the cues necessary for the production crew to execute the project.

7

Writing for the Eye

As we saw in Chapter 6, well-crafted scripts communicate a sequence of events consisting of integrated sights and sounds. The success of the nonbroadcast television writer, however, is usually in direct proportion to his or her ability to develop functional methods of *visualizing* the subject matter. At its worst, nonbroadcast programming generally fails on the visual level. Frequently this is because the subject is abstract and lacks inherent visual potential. The skilled writer looks forward to the challenges presented by difficult subject matter. Writing is problem solving, and the problem of what pictures should accompany what words is the essence of television writing.

Let's look first at typical pitfalls in writing the left side of a shooting script, then explore approaches for enhancing descriptions of what the viewer should see.

TYPICAL PROBLEMS

Verbal Dominance

Too often, nonbroadcast scripts are visually weak because the communication is driven by verbal expression. Visual expression is considered only as an afterthought, or not at all. This is not to say that all programming must be highly visual. When the purpose of the communication is to reveal the chairman or president's thinking on a critical issue facing the organization, there may be little need for visualization. Too often, however, wall-to-wall text is scripted for a narrator while only the most cursory consideration is given to what will be on the screen throughout the recitation. Strong visualization never results when the left side of the page is treated as an afterthought.

The Kitchen Sink Syndrome

The kitchen sink syndrome is just the opposite. In the writer's zeal to visualize, every narrative point has an accompanying illustration. While each visual element may be appropriate for that particular moment, there is no underlying stylistic framework or visual theme.

This problem is always compounded when the client wishes to integrate a variety of existing visuals into the program. The writer may be faced with old film footage, video tape from a previous presentation, slides from the photo library and artwork used in a promotional print piece. Each element, of course, will have been produced by different people, at different times, with no thought of the project at hand. Inexperienced writers may embrace this material and begin plugging it all into the left side of the page. Unless this is done with extreme sensitivity and skill, however, the result will be a hodgepodge of visuals lacking clarity and unity.

Inappropriate Visualization

Finally, some scripts suffer from use of visual material which is totally inappropriate. Remember, some visuals are technically inappropriate. For example, charts or graphs may contain too much information and detail for resolution on the TV screen, or a visual may be in the wrong aspect ratio for television. Writers cannot take the attitude that the director and crew will find a way around such technical problems. It's the writer's responsibility to develop a shooting script that is practical, pragmatic and "do-able." Whenever the writer paints production personnel into a corner, a disservice is done to all—especially the client.

Another form of inappropriate visualization is more stylistic. Earlier, directors were characterized by their fondness of the verb "to see." Another word directors like is "look"—used as a noun. The look of a program describes its visual style, a "documentary look," for instance, or a "high tech look." Every television program is characterized by its own individual look. Writers should keep this in mind and feel confident the look is appropriate for the specific content, audience and objectives of a project.

A serious corporate awareness program on issues relating to productivity is probably not the place for whimsical cartoon style artwork. Nor would abstract, computer-generated graphics be appropriate for a presentation that focuses on the history and heritage of an organization or institution. These examples are extreme, but there are innumerable instances of stylistic incongruity in the short history of nonbroadcast television. The writer must develop a degree of visual literacy and taste. In a studio set, for example, the distinction between wood-panelled backdrops with leather chairs versus plexiglass panels with contemporary furniture makes a definite statement about the style and culture of an organization. In describing locations, studio settings, graphics, photography, film footage, animation, special effects or any visual element, the writer should strive for a look that is compatible with the overall tone, purpose and stylistic integrity of the presentation.

GUIDELINES FOR EFFECTIVE VISUALIZATION

Make Stylistic Decisions Early

Problems such as verbal dominance or inappropriate visuals generally result from inattention to the visual style of the program in the conceptual stage. The writer can avoid many visualization problems by thinking through the visual style of the program before any narrative writing takes place. In fact, if you follow the process described in Chapter 5, you are forced to deal with what the viewer will be seeing, as well as hearing, long before you start scripting narrative copy. For the preliminary visualizing stage, you don't need to have every single graphic, camera angle or special effect clearly in mind. Rather, focus on the potential for visualization in the overall context of the program. What look and style will be both effective and appropriate?

If you envision a studio set, what elements should the set contain? What function do they perform? How are they integrated with narrator or other on-screen participants? If you're combining a variety of visual inputs, how will they be integrated so that the resulting look is unified, aesthetically whole? If you envision multiple locations or sets, what is the rationale for using each location? How are they linked together? Don't forget the relationship between visuals and voices. Is your talent on or off camera? If on camera, what environment will talent appear in? If you're suggesting totally off-camera narration, do you have sufficient visual material to engage the viewer's eye?

Sometimes, there's no simple answer to these questions. Your decisions will be influenced by content, budget considerations, production and logistical constraints, client needs—and the audience. Remember, audience predisposition toward the subject matter will affect your decisions to a great degree. By giving early consideration to the style of your visuals, you can ensure that individual shots, graphics and titles fit into the overall visual framework.

Determine the Function of Visual Material

Visuals serve many purposes in a nonbroadcast presentation. On the most literal level, you may be using the television camera to show how a task is performed, for example, in a training program on unloading liquid hydrogen. In that instance you will be quite literal in describing graphic elements. To explain the inner workings of an internal combustion engine, a program might use simple animation or a sequence of diagrams or a cutaway scale model. Such visuals serve a specific tutorial function, leading the viewer to focus on concepts, not the artwork itself. The function in all these cases is straightforward illustration.

Given other subject matter, however, visuals may be meant to create interest and stimulate the imagination, even call attention to themselves. When content is abstract, you may want visuals to serve a more presentational function. In such instances, artistic elements can be emphasized and broadly executed. Cartoon style artwork conveys an air of whimsy or humor. Computer animation, by contrast, has a high tech quality. Similarly, sets or other backdrops can range across the spectrum in terms of function. For a training program on writing the business letter, the oversized, stylized typewriter shown in Figure 7.1 provides a functional way for the narrator to refer to writing samples. But it's also a staging

Figure 7.1 The writer's description and handling of settings and backdrops should be as well conceived as narrative copy. The oversized typewriter functions as a display area for writing samples in a business correspondence course. Courtesy Crum & Forster Corporation.

device meant to be impressive and attention-getting. In wrapping management-by-objectives concepts in a folktale parody, painted backdrops capture the salt-of-the-earth flavor of folklore with bold, vivid strokes. (See Figure 7.2.) Symbols, abstractions, even "magical" electronic video effects offer still other methods of making striking visual statements.

Documentary style footage, on the other hand, may be the most functional when you seek credibility for the message. One of television's most powerful strengths is the ability to function as a window on the world, giving your audience a glimpse of realities they may not normally see. To illustrate the world of a youthful prison inmate making a new start through a special parole program, for instance, documentary footage serves the writer's purposes.

By considering carefully the *function* your visuals should perform, you can arrive at valid decisions about the *form* visual material should take. Form should evolve naturally from function. Answer the question: "What do I want visuals to *do* for the viewing audience in this program?"

Identify the Big Building Blocks

Once you have decided on the purpose and style of your visual presentation, more nuts-and-bolts considerations can be addressed. But it's still premature to start writing detailed shot descriptions. First, you need to identify the visual building blocks of your script. When toddlers construct with building blocks of different sizes, they learn to select the bigger ones first, put those in place, then add the smaller ones as the structure grows more complex. Scripting is somewhat the same. Once you have the component building blocks in mind, it's simple to write "ZOOM in for ECU on Block C. CUT to TWO SHOT of Blocks K and F..." If you've thoroughly identified the functions of your visuals, this step is simply an extension of that process.

If, for instance, you've pictured a set with multi-level staging areas as the functional method of visualizing a program on writing business letters, you next need to clarify precisely how many staging areas are needed. What is the individual purpose and function of each? How often will each area be used? How will transitions from one area to the next be accomplished? The writer should know the answer to these things before getting into the details of writing the shooting script. Or suppose you've determined that an animation sequence is a functional way to illustrate the action of a new drug. Now you need to identify how many different content points will use animation. How many animated scenes does that require? How will the scenes fit together? If you'll be visualizing principles of medical malpractice law with a sequence of short dramatic vignettes, you must determine how

Figure 7.2 Painted backdrops depict folktale locations for a management parable. The settings combine strategically placed foreground objects with much smaller paintings electronically chroma-keyed behind the talent (performers). Courtesy Crum & Forster Corporation.

many vignettes the content requires, what settings are needed (emergency room, a delivery room, etc.) and what action takes place in each locale.

At this point it's helpful to construct lists of such elements, or sketch them out in rough form, if you're one of those lucky writers who can draw. You're still not down to writing shot-by-shot descriptions nor sketching a complex storyboard. But like the toddler, play with the big blocks first, arranging them until they seem to fit together well.

In addition to helping the writer identify specific visual elements, this activity has definite practical value. If you plan to illustrate a historical narrative with still photos and period artwork, for instance, you must determine that there is sufficient source material available to sustain the piece visually. Granted, you may not know yet the sequence of these visuals, or the specific camera moves you'll script. But if you anticipate a five-minute narrative and can locate only six relevant photos or pieces of art, you're still in search of a visual solution. If the multi-level staging area set you envisioned will cost $30,000 to construct for a project budgeted at $38,000 total, you'll need to rethink the set and its elements. Again, the basis for this work should have been reflected in your treatment.

VIDEO DESCRIPTIONS

Once you've arrived at a clear perception of the style and purpose of your visuals and have the big building blocks in place, you can get down to the nitty-gritty of writing camera directions. Many beginning writers are uncertain as to just what to include in the video column of a script. Screenplay writers simply indicate locations and time of day or night in their scripts—detailed camera directions are considered amateurish.

In nonbroadcast television writing, however, where the subject matter is highly specialized and the purpose of programming goes beyond enter-tainment, it is imperative that the writer specify shots, camera angles and transitions. This doesn't mean the director will always follow such directions slavishly, nor that production logistics won't alter the writer's suggested visualization. But since almost every nonbroadcast program requires a one-of-a-kind format and visualization, it's up to the writer to include sufficient detail for the script to function as a legitimate shooting script, a working document for the production team.

Use the Video Column to Set the Stage

By all means, use the video side of the page to describe the overall function, style and look you wish to establish. Usually, this kind of video description occurs on the first page or two of a script. In the excerpt below, for instance, the writer devoted nearly an entire page to describing the style, function and component elements of a studio environment.[1]

VIDEO

FADE UP ON:

CU—Camera pans
across studio
backdrop, which
consists of flats
painted with free-style
renderings of an
office setting and
perhaps an AT&T
truck parked by
telephone pole. This
artwork is executed in
a sketchy, minimal,
free-style form. It is
not intended to be
realistic.

The art is done in
monochromatic
shades, grey and
black or tan and dark
brown, for instance.

These flats are cut out
and arranged in front
of a plain studio cyc
[or cyclorama; see
Glossary.] The
appearance is like a
life-size children's
"pop-up" art book.

---

[1]From "Sexual Harrassment: Fact or Fiction?" written by William Van Nostran, directed by James G. Libby, produced by William J. Benham for AT&T Corporate Television. Used by permission.

The same style is used
to represent two
classroom flipcharts.
Throughout the
program, the
Narrators refer to
these charts as Supers
appear in handwritten
style to highlight key
points. These
flipcharts also serve
as display areas for
getting in and out of
case study vignettes.

For this opening, the
main titles. . .

SEXUAL
HARASSMENT:
FACT OR FICTION

appear over shots of
these backdrops.
Then. . .

Cut to TWO SHOT
on male and female
Narrators. They sit on
simple stools in
foreground area.

The writer has a specific style clearly in mind and shapes that vision through text such as: ". . .executed in a sketchy, minimal, free-style form. . . not intended to be realistic. . . monochromatic shades. . ." Additionally, the writer explains how certain building blocks will be used throughout the presentation: ". . .the Narrators refer to these charts as Supers appear in handwritten style to highlight key points. These flipcharts also serve as display areas for getting in and out of vignettes."

The initial descriptions of the visual content of a program are extremely important in conveying images in the writer's mind to the client and the director. These descriptions help those all important readers of scripts to visualize the viewing experience as you intend it.

Use the Video Column to Describe Action

The writer is the first member of the production team to stage action. Although the writer's imagined actions are generally modified and refined as the production takes on a life of its own, the writer's initial indications of on-screen activity are essential. Here, for instance, are the opening shots for an employee orientation to the Maxwell House Division of General Foods.[2]

VIDEO

FADE UP ON:

Montage of shots in supermarket environment. (Could be shot from P.O.V. of shopper entering store.) We pass by check-out counter and ZOOM to can of Maxwell House being rung up. Action moves into supermarket aisles as we truck down coffee aisle.

[SUPER opening titles.]

Establish Maxwell House Sales Rep putting up display.

---

[2] From "The Best Coffee Company," written by William Van Nostran, directed by James G. Libby, produced by William Hoppe, General Foods Public Affairs, Video and Graphic Communications for the Maxwell House division. Used by permission.

Feature "The Best
Coffee Company"
slogan.

Different angle as
Narrator enters scene
and addresses camera.

Narrator strolls down
aisle, referring to shelf
facings.

Insert CLOSE-UPS
on cans and jars.

The writer uses television production terminology to describe the activity. "P.O.V." (an abbreviation for point of view) indicates that the camera should assume the vantage point of a shopper entering the store. "Truck" tells the director the camera should physically move down supermarket aisles. The writer also describes actions the on-camera participants will be performing, and calls for close-up shots as insert material. Notice that directions are specific enough that the script readers have an understanding of what shots are needed to construct the scene; at the same time, the directions provide sufficient latitude for adjusting to the logistics of the shooting environment.

Later, this same script calls for an actor to portray Joel Cheek, originator of the Maxwell House blend. He describes how he went from wholesale grocery representative working his territory on horseback in 1873 to founder of the Cheek-Neal Coffee Company, which first marketed Maxwell House. The left side of the page contains these descriptions:

VIDEO

Action begins as actor
portrays Joel Cheek.

Cheek moves about in
office with turn-of-
the-century
memorabilia. He uses
props and photo
album to illustrate his
story.

He goes to map on
wall. ZOOM to CU
on map; follow route
of Cumberland River.

MS on Cheek as he
moves to saddlebags
slung over chair.
INSERT close-ups as
he pulls coffee bean
samples from the bag.

Moves to copper
kettle and empties
samples into kettle.

INSERT close-ups of
beans as appropriate.

MS as Cheek moves
to photo album.
Begins to leaf
through. ZOOM
CU on photos or art
of Maxwell House
Hotel.

Much of this is stage business for the actor to perform. More detailed camera directions are not necessary since camera placement is a director's decision, dictated by the physical environment and ultimate blocking of stage business.

Use the Video Column to Give Camera Directions

A functional shooting script provides camera directions to the extent that they are necessary. This does not mean each and every shot will be described in the shooting script. The extent of the camera directions should correlate to the specificity required by the subject matter.

A training tape for anesthesiologists on how to administer an injection anesthetic, for instance, would call for many more specific camera directions than a dramatic vignette of an employment interview. In the case of the anesthesiology training tape, the writer would call for specific close-ups on action relating to the induction and maintenance of the anesthetic during surgery.

CU as nitrous oxide is
administered.

CU as oxygen is
administered. . .

and airway protection
provided.

ECU as muscle
relaxant injection is
administered.

Insert ECU on hand
adjusting rate of
micro-drip anesthetic.

All such specific action would be detailed in the shooting script and keyed to narrative text. In the case of the dramatic vignette, however, specific camera directions may be minimal unless there is a key bit of action or reaction that is important for the viewing audience to see at a given moment. For example:

CU on job applicant;
her face registers
confusion in response
to the interviewer's
question.

Usually, however, the blocking and staging will determine the various camera angles and cuts. Thus, as a general rule, if you want the viewing audience to see a specific image on the screen at a precise moment in the script, then describe the shot accordingly.

Use the Video Column to Indicate Titles and Supers

When you want the viewing audience to see text or other types of special graphic or visual effects, write it into the left side of the page. The superimposition of text over a scene should always be indicated by the word "SUPER." A sales training program in which track hurdles are used to symbolize the prospect's objections would be written as follows:

MS on two sales
trainees by two
hurdles.

SUPER: (Above each
hurdle)

Genuine Objection
Insincere Objection

The appearance of arrows, to draw the viewer's attention to a portion of the image, or other graphic superimpositions should be written out in a similar manner.

CU on map.

SUPER:

(Concentric circles to
indicate possible
customer service
driving routes.)

When describing superimpositions, the parentheses indicate that you are describing a visual effect as opposed to text which appears on the screen. Program titles, directions to pause or stop the tape, indentification of a speaker's name and job title are typically indicated in the left column as supers.

Use the Video Column to Describe Transitions

When your script calls for a change in location, a passage of time or a major shift in subject matter, indicate how the scenes will be bridged visually. This is especially important if the transition involves an effect other than the straight cut or camera take. If you envision a dissolve, wipe or still more complex transition, indicate the effect you have in mind on the left hand page.

Narrator walks out of
limbo area.

SUPER: titles over
black.

DISSOLVE TO:

MS on two sales
trainees in studio
environment
containing hurdles
and flats with stadium
artwork.

In this example, the dissolve indicates the transition between a change in on-camera participants as well as environments.

Use the Video Column to Describe Special Effects

When the writer feels an electronic video effect is critical to telling the story, the effect should be described in the left hand column. Visual devices such as chroma-key or digital effects such as squeeze zooms, halls of mirrors and tumbling pictures need to be described in as much detail as necessary for the production team to execute the effect.

Special effects should never be used for the sake of effect. When clearly motivated by content or stylistic decisions, however, they should be described as precisely as possible in the left hand column.

Graphic simulating
aperture of a camera
lens. Matte title
graphic, "Focus on
Research" in center.

Simulate closing and
opening shutter. Scene
of new R and D con-
struction is now matted
into the shutter area.

Some visual effects, such as the above, are difficult to describe with text. For this reason, the writer should make a point of discussing the function and substance of an effect with the director and technicians who are required to execute the effect.

SUMMARY: KEEP IT FUNCTIONAL

Remember, the purpose of the left side of the page is to communicate the sequence of visual events that will comprise the viewing experience. You need to supply sufficient instructions so that client and crew understand how the content will be visualized. You must also use the language of television production as a shorthand to communicate how the left hand page should be excuted. Descriptions of screen action, camera shots and video effects represent a practical, pragmatic kind of writing. Keep video instructions functional and realistic. If you have a clear perception of visual style and content before writing detailed shot descriptions, you should find the page-by-page writing flows logically from image to image. As you gain experience anticipating and solving visualization problems before they develop, you'll find first draft shooting scripts will have an inherent cohesiveness and unity that stamp them as the work of a professional television writer.

8

Writing For The Ear

For the right side of the split-page script, one fact is paramount: words on paper are eventually given life by a human voice. Narration is read only by a handful of people: the client, producer/director, audio engineer and, of course, the narrator. The viewing audience reads nothing. They listen. Although later chapters deal with techniques for interview and dramatic formats, the fact remains that nonbroadcast television is heavy on straightforward, explanatory narration. Writers need to become proficient at scripting vivid narrative copy that communicates ideas with verbal and *aural* clarity. In most cases, the viewing audience will hear your words only once and at a predetermined pace. Thus, developing a narrative style that plays to the ear is crucial.

Writing for the ear is really not all that difficult. It just requires some common sense—like don't write more than can be spoken in a single breath. The guidelines that follow are offered as practical pointers. If you have not had a lot of practice at scripting narration, you'll need to think consciously about applying these principles. As you gain experience, a functional narrative style should become second nature.

NARRATIVE TYPES

At the start, you must know which of the three basic types of narration you will be using. Of these, the first two can be treated with a similar stylistic approach. First is the professional on-camera spokesperson. The professional, although carrying the liability of being an outsider in programs often designed to communicate inside information, has the distinct advantage of being able to read narrative copy so it sounds conversational and not stilted. Thus, whenever detailed content points need to be delivered precisely, the professional narrator is the best choice. Second is the off-camera spokesperson, the visuals and voices format referred to in Chapter 5. An unseen narrator merely comments on the screen action as opposed to being a visible participant. Here too, the professional voice is almost always preferred. When there is no face with the voice, expression must come solely from vocal inflection, which requires special performing abilities.

In writing purely informational copy for the on- or off-camera professional, the writer's style should be direct and purposeful. While some nuances in personal style are appropriate, purely informational programming should be objective and factual. The writer's voice is transparent, reflecting no editorial or personal bias. (The style for motivational programming or comedic/dramatic approaches is different. For now, we're focusing on expository narration.)

The third narrative type, however, does call for a personal style—not the writer's, but the speaker's. The in-house spokesperson should be used when *who* delivers the message carries as much or more weight than the specific content. When the president or other executive in an organization talks, people listen because of the individual's position. In contrast to the professional narrator, the in-house spokesperson's message should be totally in keeping with the managerial style of the individual. This is more like traditional speech writing. The writer "ghosts" for the busy executive, and has to have sufficient personal knowledge and insight into the boss's character to express ideas in a tone compatible with that individual's personal style. Later in the chapter we'll look at some specific suggestions for doing this.

With these types in mind, let's discuss several guidelines for writing for the ear.

OBSERVE *THE ELEMENTS OF STYLE*

Strunk and White's *The Elements of Style* is still the accepted standard on brevity, clarity and good English usage, and its principles certainly apply to scripting narration. My advice: commit *The Elements of Style* to memory; it's a model of brevity in its own right. (More practically, at least read Strunk and White about twice a year to keep its principles of good English usage fresh in your mind.)

Three of Professor Strunk's stylistic rules have special relevance for writers of narration. First. . .

Use the active voice.
The active voice is usually more direct and vigorous than the passive.[1]

Direct, vigorous writing has greater impact on the ear than vague,

---

[1] William Strunk Jr. and E.B. White, *The Elements of Style,* third edition (New York: Macmillan Publishing Co., Inc., 1979), p.18.

indefinite passive constructions. The active voice gives the writer of narration a better shot at aural clarity.

Second. . .

Put statements in positive form.
Make definite assertions. . . If your every sentence admits a doubt, your writing will lack authority.[2]

Nonbroadcast television plays to captive audiences who expect to receive useful information or to learn new skills. The more positive and forceful your narration, the more likely the viewing audience will feel they are receiving a positive, worthwhile communication. Writing that lacks authority is not worth the expense of mounting a video production. It also places the narrator—your flesh and blood transmitter—in the awkward position of sounding wishy-washy.

Finally. . .

Omit needless words.
Vigorous writing is concise. A sentence should contain no unnecessary words. . . This requires not that the writer make all his sentences short, or that he avoid all detail and treat his subjects only in outline, but that every word tell.[3]

When you are writing narration, words translate into screen time, which in turn translates into money. In a medium which can gobble up time and money, the writer owes it to audience and producer to be economical in every sense. Become ruthless, and "omit needless words."

Observe these three principles, and you've taken a big step toward ensuring that your own narration can be spoken easily and will be clear to the listening audience.

KEEP IT CONVERSATIONAL

Narrators in voice-over sessions are often directed: "Keep it conversational." The admonition should be applied first to the scriptwriter. Conversational tone begins with the writing. A narrator can't take convoluted, formal text and make it sound like a chat over the back fence simply by reading with a big smile and sounding friendly. The following principles characterize a conversational style.

---

[2]Ibid, pp. 19-20.
[3]Ibid, p. 23.

Conversational Writing is Informal and Personal

Even when television is viewed in groups, the psychological dynamics of a one-to-one personal communication are at play. Unlike a speech, which addresses a group using rhetorical and declamatory conventions, good television narration is written as a conversation directed to an audience of one. So write the way people speak. That doesn't mean narration should be riddled with slang or take on the random structure of a spontaneous conversation. But it should convey informality and have a personal tone, as though the narrator is speaking to an individual.

As an example, here are two versions of the same information. The copy on the left contains legal jargon, which often crops up in nonbroadcast projects. While this may be marginally acceptable in print, it becomes totally sterile and impersonal when read aloud. (Go ahead—try to read that copy aloud and sound friendly and personal.) The version on the right, by contrast, is written as one person might express the thought in conversation with another person.

To qualify for an allowance, all advertising must be prepared in accordance with the terms and conditions of the current Cooperative Advertising Agreement. . .	To receive your allowance, make sure ads conform to requirements spelled out in the current Co-Op Ad Allowance Agreement. . .

Several factors make the right-hand version more appropriate for a narrator to read conversationally. First, it uses personal pronouns, "you" and "your," acknowledging that the comment is directed to individuals. Longer words, such as "advertising" and cooperative," are shortened to a conversational form: "ad" and "co-op." The legal tone of the phrases such as "in accordance with" or "terms and conditions" is simplified through a less threatening vocabulary: "conform to requirements." Notice also the conversational version "omits needless words."

Develop an ear for the simplicity which characterizes spoken conversation. Contractions and simplified word forms, for instance, lend informality to narrative copy.

Instead of	Write
we will	we'll
cannot	can't
automobile	auto/car
due to the fact that	because

Use the Language of the Audience

On the surface, this suggestion may seem to contradict earlier advice to use the simplified, straightforward word form. In reality, however, it recognizes that audiences of insiders often have their own trade or professional shorthand. The writer's initial research should include developing a working knowledge of that professional or industry lingo. For instance, in the insurance industry, otherwise common words such as "risk," "exposures" or "surplus" have unique connotations. In the pharmaceutical/medical community, words and phrases like "efficacy," "indications," "over-the-counter," "well tolerated" and "mode of action" all carry specific meanings.

However, when the communication is directed to an outside audience—the general public, opinion leaders or other industry outsiders—then special terminology should be avoided or properly explained. The conversational standard, then, is determined not by the writer or the client but by the audience.

Avoid Hyperbole and Hype

Bold claims and superlatives belong to the advertising copywriter. When your audience consists of employees, stockholders, a student body or faculty, physicians, lawyers, nurses or other specialists, straight talk and logic make for the most credible message. If you want a narrator to sound sincere, knowledgeable and convincing, then write narration that is sincere, knowledgeable and convincing.

This doesn't mean you can't tout a product or generate enthusiasm for a new policy or program. But substantiate positive sentences and claims by offering proof that a product or program is the "best on the market." Sales representatives need real features and benefits and hard data to make a good sales presentation. They also need to be prepared for marketplace realities. Selling the sizzle in place of the steak usually leaves the audience hungry for more.

Write With Pictures in Mind

Words without pictures are just a speech. You can't make your narration functional by writing in a vacuum. Once again, don't write anything on the right side of the page without knowing what's taking place on the left side. The most obvious reason for this is to avoid audio-visual redundancy—describing through narration what is perfectly obvious visually. Narrative copy should expand the visual portion of the presentation, adding perspective and interpretive viewpoints.

But it's also important to be aware of the visual content in order to make the most of the medium. As an example, take a presentation on arthritis designed to support the introduction of a new drug therapy. The sample opening narration is symptomatic of a writer who is thinking only verbally.

> THIS PROGRAM HAS BEEN
> PREPARED TO PROVIDE
> INFORMATION ABOUT ARTHRITIS
> AND TO SHOW HOW OUR NEW ANTI-
> ARTHRITIC COMPOUND FITS INTO
> THE THERAPEUTIC MARKETPLACE.
>
> ARTHRITIS IS A DISEASE WHICH
> AFFECTS THE JOINTS. THE DISEASE
> CAN TAKE MANY FORMS BUT IS
> CHARACTERIZED BY AN
> INFLAMMATION WHICH LEAVES
> THE JOINT STIFF AND IMMOBILE.

What's missing here is any sense of visual potential or synergism between words and pictures. It reads like a speech and suggests nothing more than a talking head lecture. Compare that narrative copy to the vigor of a narration written to play against a strong visual story line, as in the following excerpt.[4]

VIDEO	AUDIO
FADE UP:	
On X-ray photo-graphy footage show-ing movement of limbs.	**NARRATOR**: THE HUMAN JOINT—A NETWORK OF CONNECTIVE TISSUE WHICH LINKS BONE TO BONE AND GIVES MAN FREEDOM OF MOVE-MENT.
Tight on female nar-rator in park locale.	WHEN THE HUMAN JOINT FUNC-TIONS PROPERLY, IT WORKS

---

[4]From "Meclomen: A Unique Compound," written by William Van Nostran, directed by James G. Libby, produced by the O'Hara Company for Parke-Davis Co., a division of Warner-Lambert, Inc. Used by permission.

Narrator is in 40's; yet has youthful air. Most important, should have "presence" to speak with authority. During this first line, shot widens to reveal athletic activity (guys tossing football or throwing frisbee).	EXCEEDINGLY WELL. . .
CU—On athletic activity. Feature joints as examples of flexibility.	MAN IN MOTION MAY BE POWER-FUL AND ATHLETIC. . .
Tight on Narrator, Different Angle show-ing woman on park bench in background.	YET OUR JOINTS ALSO GIVE US THE DEXTERITY TO MOVE WITH PRECI-SION. . .
Cut to CU of woman on park bench knit-ting sweater. Feature hands.	SO THAT "MAN IN MOTION" MAY ALSO BE NIMBLE AND QUICK.
CU—On Narrator, Different Angle.	BUT THE HUMAN JOINT DOESN'T ALWAYS FUNCTION JUST AS IT SHOULD. IT'S SUSCEPTIBLE TO DISEASE, AND WHENEVER THE HUMAN JOINT BECOMES INFLAMED. . .
Insert tight shot of athlete.	WHAT ONCE MOVED FLUIDLY AND EFFORTLESSLY. . .
Cut to lady walking with cane. Insert detail of hand. She reaches park bench and slowly takes a a seat.	TURNS STIFF, PAINFUL, IMMOBILE. INFLAMMATION OF THE JOINT IS SUCH A COMMON MALADY THAT MILLIONS OF AMERICANS ARE AFFECTED TO ONE DEGREE OR ANOTHER. WE CALL IT ARTHRITIS.

Here the narration works only in the context of the specific visuals. Be sure you write narration with a firm knowledge of what the visuals will be.

Don't Over-Write

The right side of the page is not just for words. It's labelled audio, which also includes music and sound effects. When writing for the ear, keep in mind that, at certain strategic points, it's most effective to allow the narrator to step aside for a musical or sound effect interlude. Sometimes, the best accompaniment to a visual is nothing more than silence.

Test Your Copy

The acid test for narrative copy is foolproof: read it aloud. This is the quickest, surest way to detect narrative problems and fix them. If you as the writer can't read the copy comfortably, something's wrong. For instance, read this copy aloud right now.

> OUR NEW "SNEEZE" COMMERCIAL
> WILL BURST INTO THE HOMES OF
> MILLIONS OF AMERICANS
> STARTING THE WEEK OF
> NOVEMBER SECOND AND WILL
> IMPACT ON THE COLD AND FLU
> TARGET AUDIENCE THROUGH A
> MIX OF PRIME TIME, LATE NIGHT
> AND DAYTIME EXPOSURE AT THE
> ONSET OF THE COLD AND FLU
> SEASON.

A third of the way through it leaves one gasping for breath. It also makes two references to a specific time frame: "November second" and the "cold and flu season." Here's one possible rewrite.

> OUR NEW "SNEEZE" COMMERCIAL
> WILL BURST INTO THE HOMES OF
> MILLIONS OF AMERICANS
> STARTING THE WEEK OF
> NOVEMBER SECOND. AT THE ONSET
> OF THE COLD AND FLU SEASON,
> THE COMMERCIAL WILL REACH
> THE TARGET AUDIENCE THROUGH

A MIX OF PRIME TIME, LATE NIGHT
AND DAYTIME EXPOSURE.

Now, see if that isn't easier to read conversationally. Also, the connection between "November second" and the "cold and flu" season is now clarified—yet we've omitted the duplication of the phrase.

Even better than reading to yourself, sit down with the producer or director to read your first draft aloud, making notes about what needs improvement. The script excerpt in Figure 8.1 is annotated and then rewritten to illustrate points we've been discussing. Read both versions aloud and notice the difference. The revised version not only uses fewer words and relies more heavily on visual storytelling but also makes more liberal and functional use of music to cue transitions. Most significant, however, there is a synergistic interaction between the left and right sides of the page, a sense of unity and compatibility.

COPY FOR THE NONPROFESSIONAL NARRATOR

Certainly, the same stylistic elements that guide the writing of narration apply when writing for the executive or other nonprofessionals. In fact, it's even more important to ensure that the copy is written to be spoken. The trained professional can adapt to an unusually long sentence or successfully navigate a tongue-twisting phrase. But the nonprofessional must have copy that can be spoken in a normal, conversational manner and that suits the style of the speaker.

When scripting for an executive, then, the writer must learn about the personality and style of the executive and adopt a fitting tone. Find out whether you're dealing with an executive who's strong and forceful, a captain of industry or one who comes across as one of the boys, folksy and down-to-earth. Is the executive one who takes a rational, reasoned approach to the business or a highly motivational leader who appeals to the emotions? The staff writer usually has advantages over the freelancer in these cases. Yet, even in-house writers are often isolated from busy executives. Both staff and freelance writers should try to review an executive's past speeches and video appearances to get a feel for rhetorical style. It's also important to meet with the executive, even if only for 15 to 20 minutes, to hear firsthand what the executive would like to accomplish.

If you're scripting for a content expert, your role is to help that person express his or her knowledge through television. In addition to gaining insights into personality, consider what visual support will help convey content. Will the person work best with physical props, or will cutaway graphics prove more functional?

**Figure 8.1: Sample Script with Comments on and Revision of Audio
Portion for More Effective Audio-Visual Presentation***

VIDEO	AUDIO
	(Print Version)
Colonial Williamsburg footage featuring individual artisans: wheelwright, silversmith, basket weaver, bookbinder.	**MUSIC**: (18th Century recorder melody.)
	OFF-CAMERA NARRATOR: THIS IS HISTORIC WILLIAMSBURG, VIRGINIA. HERE, A VARIETY OF CRAFTSMEN— FROM SILVERSMITHS TO BLACK- SMITHS TO POTTERS AND WHEEL- WRIGHTS—ALL PLY THEIR TRADE TO PRODUCE A WIDE RANGE OF HANDCRAFTED GOODS.
	THESE ARTISANS MUST TAKE PRIDE IN THEIR WORK AND DERIVE GREAT PERSONAL SATISFACTION IN THE PRODUCTS THEY MAKE.
DISSOLVE TO:	BUT IN THIS DAY AND AGE, MOST PEOPLE DO NOT HAVE THE LUXURY
Footage from Extracorporeal's Tampa Bay Plant showing close- ups of assembly operations.	TO MAKE PRODUCTS ONE AT A TIME.

*From "The Extra Care Story: A Quality Circle Case Study," written by William Van Nostran, directed and produced by John Sheahan, Johnson & Johnson Worldwide Video Network, copyright 1982. (Distributed through Films, Inc.) Used by permission.

Figure 8.1: Sample Script with Comments on and Revision of Audio Portion for More Effective Audio-Visual Presentation

COMMENTS	AUDIO (Audio-Visual Version)
	MUSIC: (18th Century recorder melody.)

To identify location, all that's necessary is the SUPER:
    WILLIAMSBURG, VIRGINIA
      TIME: THE PRESENT
Unnecessary detail; wordy.
	OFF-CAMERA NARRATOR: ONE OF THE FEW PLACES LEFT IN AMERICA WHERE ESSENTIAL GOODS ARE HANDCRAFTED.

Wishy-washy. Put statements in positive form.	USING TRADITIONAL METHODS, TOOLS AND MATERIALS, ARTISANS AT WILLIAMSBURG SEE REFLECTIONS OF THEIR OWN INDIVIDUALITY IN THE PRODUCTS THEY MAKE.
Poor transitional device. Lacks clarity. Use of word "luxury" is inappropriate—the topic is productivity and quality.	**MUSICAL SEGUE**: (To contemporary rock theme.) **NARRATOR**: TODAY, MOST PEOPLE MAKE PRODUCTS IN ENVIRONMENTS LIKE THIS: EXTRACORPOREAL'S TAMPA BAY PLANT—WHERE SOPHISTICATED KIDNEY DIALYSIS MACHINES ARE MANUFACTURED.

(continued on next page)

Figure 8.1: Sample Script with Comments on and Revision of Audio Portion for More Effective Audio-Visual Presentation (cont.)

VIDEO	AUDIO (Print Version)
	IN THE 1980s, MOST OF THE WORK-FORCE MANUFACTURES PRODUCTS IN ENVIRONMENTS WHICH STRESS EFFICIENCY, STANDARDIZATION, QUALITY AND PRODUCTIVE OUTPUT.
	THIS PLANT, FOR INSTANCE, IS LOCATED IN TAMPA, FLORIDA. THE EXTRACORPOREAL COMPANY MAKES SOPHISTICATED, LIFE-SUSTAINING KIDNEY DIALYSIS MACHINES—USED BY PATIENTS WHO SUFFER FROM END STAGE RENAL DISEASE. THIS PLANT, LIKE THOUSANDS OF OTHERS ACROSS THE COUNTRY, USES AN ASSEMBLY-LINE APPROACH.
DISSOLVE TO: Montage of Ford assembly line footage showing man pulling auto followed by closer shots on workers.	THIS CONCEPT, AS EVERYONE KNOWS, GOES BACK TO THE PIONEERING INFLUENCE OF HENRY FORD. THIS HISTORIC FORD FOOT-AGE CLEARLY DEMONSTRATES UNI-VERSAL PRINCIPLES OF MASS PRO-DUCTION—IN WHICH THERE'S AN INTERCHANGEABLE ORGANIZATION BETWEEN MAN, MATERIALS AND MACHINE.
Montage of industrial footage showing a variety of manufactur-ing operations, all relating to assembly-line technology.	OTHER INDUSTRIES SOON FOUND OUT THAT BY ADAPTING THESE SAME ASSEMBLY-LINE TECHNIQUES TO MAKE A VAST ARRAY OF PRO-DUCTS. . . FROM WASHING MACHINES . . .TO ELECTRONICS. . . AND PHARMACEUTICALS. . . THEY, TOO,

Figure 8.1: Sample Script with Comments on and Revision of Audio Portion for More Effective Audio-Visual Presentation (cont.)

COMMENTS	AUDIO (Audio-Visual Version)
This passage is too dense verbally for good narrative copy. The visuals themselves should suggest "efficiency, standardization," etc.	
The term "renal" may not be familiar to all audience members. It's probably too much detail at this point, anyway.	THE PLANT IS ORGANIZED FOR MASS PRODUCTION USING FAMILIAR ASSEMBLY-LINE CONCEPTS. PLANTS AND FACTORIES OF TODAY OWE THEIR HERITAGE NOT SO MUCH TO COLONIAL WILLIAMSBURG, AS TO HENRY FORD'S ASSEMBLY LINES.
Again, this passage is too wordy. Make the point—then move on.	**MUSICAL SEGUE**: (To turn-of-the-century theme.) **NARRATOR**: PRIMITIVE BY TODAY'S STANDARDS, THE PRINCIPLES OF MASS PRODUCTION ARE CLEARLY IN EVIDENCE IN THIS HISTORIC FOOT-AGE. THE ASSEMBLY LINE DERIVES ITS MUSCLE FROM THE INTER-CHANGEABLE ORGANIZATION OF MAN, MATERIALS AND MACHINE. **MUSICAL SEGUE**: (To contemporary, up tempo theme.)
Read this sentence aloud and its structural faults become imme-diately apparent.	**NARRATOR**: OTHER INDUSTRIES WERE QUICK TO ADOPT ASSEMBLY-LINE TECHNIQUES TO MAKE A VAST ARRAY OF PRODUCTS. . . FROM WASHING MACHINES. . . TO ELEC-TRONICS. . . AND PHARMACEUTICALS.

(continued on next page)

Figure 8.1: Sample Script with Comments on and Revision of Audio Portion for More Effective Audio-Visual Presentation (cont.)

VIDEO	AUDIO (Print Version)
	COULD PROFIT FROM THE BENE-FITS OF ASSEMBLY-LINE TECH-NIQUES.
	ALL ACROSS THE LAND, THE STANDARD OF LIVING ROSE AS INDUSTRY BECAME MORE AND MORE PRODUCTIVE.
Final footage in sequence goes to slow motion; then stops on a freeze frame. This is followed by a series of freeze frame stills from contemporary assembly lines, paced to the narration.	BUT TODAY, THERE TENDS TO BE AN AIR OF SKEPTICISM, EVEN A CON-CERN, OVER THE PRODUCTIVITY AND QUALITY OF OUR PLANTS AND FACTORIES. CONSUMERS ARE CON-CERNED; EVEN BUSINESSMEN THEM-SELVES.
Stills or animated slides showing Japanese products in American showrooms.	IN MANY INDUSTRIES, PRODUCTS IMPORTED FROM OVERSEAS WERE PROVIDING A LOT OF COMPETITION FOR AMERICAN INDUSTRY.
Stills showing Japanese Quality Circles.	BUT IN THIS PROGRAM, WE'RE NOT GOING TO LOOK AT IMPORTED PRO-DUCTS—BUT AT THE WAY IN WHICH JAPANESE FIRMS USE PARTICIPA-TORY MANAGEMENT AND WORKER INVOLVEMENT TO SOLVE PROBLEMS THROUGH A CONCEPT KNOWN AS THE QUALITY CIRCLE.
DISSOLVE TO: Action footage from Tampa plant, including shots of Quality Circles in action.	FOR THE NEXT SEVERAL MINUTES, WE'LL EXPLORE THE IMPACT OF QUALITY CIRCLES ON EMPLOYEES WHO WORK FOR EXTRACORPOREAL IN TWO TAMPA LOCATIONS.

Figure 8.1: Sample Script with Comments on and Revision of Audio Portion for More Effective Audio-Visual Presentation (cont.)

COMMENTS	AUDIO (Audio-Visual Version)
	IT RESULTED IN THE HIGHEST INDUS-TRIAL OUTPUT AND STANDARD OF LIVING ANYWHERE IN THE WORLD.
Abrupt transition. Furthermore, the writer loses impact by qualify-ing with words like "tends" and "even." Put statements in positive form.	BUT THEN. . . SLOWLY, ALMOST IMPERCEPTIBLY SOMETHING WENT WRONG. CONSUMERS QUESTIONED THE QUALITY OF PRODUCTS "MADE IN AMERICA." BUSINESSMEN QUES-TIONED THE PRODUCTIVE OUTPUT OF THEIR OWN PLANTS.
Redundant. "Imported" and "over-seas" are synomonous in this con-text.	IN MANY INDUSTRIES, IMPORTED PRODUCTS SEEMED BETTER BUILT, OFFERING MORE VALUE FOR THE DOLLAR. THIS REPORT, IN FACT, CENTERS ON A JAPANESE IMPORT.
An interesting contrast between importing products and manage-ment techniques is not fully ex-ploited. The writing can be made more vigorous by being more direct.	NOT A CAR OR A TV—BUT A FORM OF PARTICIPATORY MANAGEMENT AND WORKER INVOLVEMENT KNOWN AS THE QUALITY CIRCLE.
The phrase, "For the next several minutes" does nothing to forward the narrative thread. Omit need-less words and phrases.	WE'LL EXPLORE THE IMPACT OF QUALITY CIRCLES ON THE 170 MEN AND WOMEN WHO WORK IN TWO EXTRACORPOREAL TAMPA LOCA-TIONS.

Generally, the role of the nonprofessional should be limited and clearly defined. An executive may provide opening or closing commentary to put detailed content in context. Content experts may lend credibility to a presentation by introducing major concepts. Detailed content, however, is usually best suited to delivery by professional talent. In sum, when writing copy for nonprofessionals, keep it brief, functional and suited to their personalities.

CONCLUSION: PUTTING IT ALL TOGETHER

The writer's task is to develop picture and sound combinations that best communicate content to the target audience. You can't script meaningful narration without full knowledge of the visuals involved. And the combined visual and narrative style must be appropriate to subject, audience and purpose. The final script excerpt in this chapter illustrates once more how visuals and narration should play off one another. The content is quite abstract: the benefits of an annuity plan to potential investors. The writer could have set the action in a limbo studio environment but chose instead to use real exterior locations. Pay close attention to the description of setting and background action. Look for symbolic meaning, even in quite realistic visuals.[5]

VIDEO	AUDIO
Scene 1—Wall Street exterior.	
Fade up on:	
ECU—on Wall Street sign, ZOOM out to reveal Narrator.	NARRATOR: THIS IS WALL STREET. AND IF YOU'RE LIKE MOST DEAN WITTER REYNOLDS CLIENTS, YOU'VE COME TO US FOR HELP IN MAKING SOUND INVESTMENTS IN STOCKS AND OTHER SECURITIES.

---

[5]From "The Perfect Serious $ Solution," written and produced by William Van Nostran and directed by James G. Libby for Dean Witter Reynolds and Crum & Forster Corporation. Copyright Crum & Forster Corporation, 1978, 1982. Used by permission.

Different Angle, as Narrator walks down street. Comes to triangular traffic sign prepared for display of graphics.

AND, LIKE MOST CLIENTS, THIS TRIANGLE COULD WELL REPRESENT YOUR OWN INVESTMENT PROFILE. . .

ECU—On traffic sign, which serves as investment triangle graphic. POP-ON TITLE: "RISK" [In top third of triangle.]

THE TOP OF YOUR INVESTMENT TRIANGLE REPRESENTS THAT PORTION OF YOUR MONEY YOU'RE WILLING TO SPECULATE WITH. THESE INVESTMENTS OFFER POTENTIAL FOR A HIGH RETURN— BUT WITH AN EQUALLY HIGH RISK ELEMENT.

ECU—On traffic sign. POP-ON TITLE: "BLUE CHIP" [In middle of triangle.]

IT'S LIKELY THE GREATEST SHARE OF YOUR INVESTMENTS ARE DEVOTED TO A BALANCED PORT-FOLIO OF BLUE CHIPS—OFFERING STEADY GROWTH OVER THE LONG HAUL.

Scene 2—Upper middle class suburban street scene.

ECU—on street sign, Narrator enters frame. POP-ON TITLE: "SERIOUS $"

BUT THE BASE OF YOUR INVEST-MENT TRIANGLE IS WHAT WE'LL CALL YOUR "SERIOUS MONEY."

Narrator begins to stroll down tree-lined street.

IT'S THE KIND OF MONEY YOU DON'T TAKE CHANCES WITH. YOU WANT TO BE SURE IT'S THERE WHEN YOU NEED IT.

Passes neighbor, working on lawn.

IT'S MONEY SET ASIDE FOR THE PROVERBIAL "RAINY DAY"

Narrator refers to background action— teenagers tossing football.	OR TO HELP FOOT THE KIDS' COLLEGE EXPENSES. . .
Woman rides up driveway on bicycle.	HELP WITH YOUR OWN RETIRE-MENT, OR ANY NUMBER OF IMPORTANT PURPOSES.
Narrator stops; camera goes slowly tighter.	BUT RIGHT NOW—YOUR "SERIOUS MONEY" IS IN "DOUBLE JEOPARDY"—BATTERED BY THE DUAL EFFECT OF HIGH INFLATION AND HIGH TAXES. . .

The writer has described the settings and background with such detail because of their symbolic potential to enhance the effect of the spoken word. Once again, there's a synergy between left and right sides of the page. Solid expository scenes that use a specific visual style and strong, positive narrative copy are the cornerstone of nonbroadcast scriptwriting. For most projects, this will be all that's needed, but there will be times when other narrative techniques are more appropriate. The next three chapters explore more specialized program formats.

9

Writing Unscripted Formats

For most clients, there's safety in a fully scripted program. There are no surprises. Every word is down on paper, meticulously approved prior to shooting. Visuals can be checked, revised, perfected. The fully scripted program is also easier on the director and the production team. The director knows precisely how many locations, scenes, set-ups and shots are required. With thorough pre-production planning, shooting and editing can go literally by the numbers. For cut-and-dried factual content, a fully scripted format is probably the most economical.

Such rigidly scripted and produced formats, however, are not always the best way to achieve objectives. For many nonbroadcast topics, the story is best told not by a writer but by "real people," appearing on camera as themselves. Properly executed, the resulting program exudes a reality and credibility that is unattainable with fully scripted formats. This sincerity is particularly appropriate for issue-oriented programming when the subject involves controversy, when there are shades of grey and room for honest differences of opinion.

THE UNSCRIPTED FORMAT

Perhaps the most common unscripted program is the traditional interview. For example, the chairman of the board's response to questions about the rationale for a new acquisition may be the ideal way to provide information to all employees and clear the air of rumors.

Such interviews can take many forms. The most straightforward approach is a one-on-one interview with someone posing a series of questions to the subject. In the Barbara Walters style of interview, the interviewer has the responsibility of both asking the right questions and insuring the interview has direction, focus and clarity. Although generally condensed through editing, this type of unscripted programming has an inherent continuity—a definite beginning, middle and end.

In planning the interview format certain fundamental issues need to be addressed. The first question is who will conduct the interview. Outside professional talent may be ideal in terms of asking prepared questions, but, unless issues are broad in scope, the outsider will not possess the insight needed for follow-up questioning. If a group of employees can be gathered as a studio audience, questions could come directly from the floor, and, instead of a single interview subject, several executives or experts might answer as a panel or executive forum. If representative employees are chosen to ask the questions, however, they may be intimidated and fail to pose hard questions of people in authority.

The Documentary Style Program

Analogous to the classic documentary is a more involved unscripted format for which the writer provides overall structure, narrative and editorial direction. Since nonbroadcast programs are produced to meet the communication needs of an organization, the objective reporting and editorial aloofness of the pure documentary are usually inappropriate. Also, the strong presence of an on-camera reporter as in commercial documentaries tends to be too obtrusive for the nonbroadcast style. Therefore, this chapter concentrates on an unscripted, documentary style format that makes use of off-camera narration. While interviews remain the vehicle for telling the story, the focus is always on the interviewee—not the interviewer and not the narrator.

For this documentary style program, diverse viewpoints from a variety of sources are needed to tell the story comprehensively. An off-camera interviewer makes it easy to weave individual responses into an overall structure. Questions are phrased so the subject's responses can be selectively edited and combined with the remarks of others on the same topic. Camera angles focus solely on the subject, and the interviewer's questions wind up on the cutting room floor. Thirty seconds may be all that's selected from a 20-minute interview. Or a number of short responses from a long interview may be interspersed with other comments or narrative links as appropriate. Continuity derives not from any one interview, but from the selective use of varied interview footage combined with narrative and cutaway footage to illuminate a specific point of view.

The unscripted format analyzed in this chapter, then, has the following characteristics:

- It often uses off-camera narration to establish major themes and provide transitional bridges between subjects.

- The bulk of the content is communicated through interview footage.

- Off-camera interviewer's questions are edited out, permitting random use of interview footage.

- Comments from various individuals are edited together in patchwork fashion.

The Writer's Role

The writer's role in such projects, particularly in the area of pre-production planning, can often prove as intense and demanding as more traditional assignments. This stems from the psychological dynamics of the unscripted production environment, in which success requires gaining the confidence of a variety of people. Obviously, interview subjects will not speak freely and informatively unless they feel a sense of trust. But equally important is management's sense of trust. The unscripted production process contradicts management's ingrained approval imperative. Corporate executives or college and hospital administrators find comfort and security in established approval processes for print and fully scripted programs. Producing the unscripted program, however, means management must make an act of faith. The producer must seek approval to spend dollars and expose many individuals to the trauma of appearing on camera in advance of developing a script.

The writer can make an invaluable contribution at this juncture, instilling a sense of confidence through pre-production planning documents, which chart a direction and provide a focus for the project. Beyond that, the writer often functions as a critical ear during interview taping sessions or, in some cases, even performs the interviewing tasks. (Writers should be good interviewers.) Once footage is in the can, the writer should participate in the process of selecting appropriate interview comments and fashioning the viewing experience. In documentary production, writing narration generally occurs after the interviews are shot and the overall structure is fleshed out by interweaving suitable interview comments.

In scripted formats, the writer's role is heavily weighted toward pre-production. In an unscripted program, the writer may be involved from pre-production through production into post-production. We'll explore the writer's involvement in each of these phases and point out differences from the scripted production process.

PRE-PRODUCTION

To contribute conceptually and creatively to an unscripted program, early involvement is essential. Even though word-for-word narration will not be written until after shooting, the same preliminary research, objective setting and conceptual work that goes into scripted programs should be undertaken.

Research

The writer's research agenda for an unscripted project will start with the same content-oriented focus used in researching a fully scripted program. In fact, quite often, the writer begins research not knowing whether content and objectives will suggest a scripted or unscripted treatment.

In this chapter, we'll follow an unscripted project from start to finish. The program, produced for the Johnson & Johnson Worldwide Video Network, and subsequently distributed by Films, Inc., focuses on the success story of Quality Circles at Extracorporeal's Tampa Bay plant, one of the Johnson & Johnson family of companies.[1] (Extracorporeal manufactures kidney dialysis machines, including products designed for treatment in the patient's home.) The first research task was to find out what a Quality Circle is and how it works. In fact, a Quality Circle is a form of participatory management: workers meet in small groups and use structured techniques to identify and solve common problems. Its success in Japan prompted interest in the concept among U.S. managers as a way to improve quality and productivity.

Once the producer or writer senses that an unscripted format may be the optimum way to tell the story, the research focus shifts to pre-interviews with potential on-camera participants. The writer (and often the producer) listens carefully not only to what is said but to how it is said. Does the individual speak with conviction? Does the person communicate with facial expression and gesture as well as words? Is there a sense of personal involvement and experience? How will members of the target audience relate to this individual?

The writer also begins to envision how each individual fits into the fabric of the entire story. What part of the story is *this* person qualified to tell? In the documentary on a Quality Circle success story, the perspectives of the plant manager, middle management, supervisors and production workers are likely to be quite different and distinct. Yet all viewpoints need expression to tell a balanced story. So in this research, the writer is looking for both factual content and the way in which each individual's personal

---

[1]"The Extra Care Story: A Quality Circle Case Study," written by William Van Nostran, directed and produced by John Sheahan. Copyright 1982. Used by permission.

Showing scenes from real life is one of the strengths of the documentary style program. Sheet metal workers at Extracorporeal meeting in an actual session illustrate the value of Quality Circles better than could narration or other scripted material. Courtesy Johnson and Johnson.

experiences and viewpoints reflect or illuminate content issues. Simultaneously, the writer assesses each individual's capability to communicate candidly and credibly on camera.

Again, trust must be established with each person who appears before the camera. Aside from those few self-proclaimed hams, most people are reluctant to face a television camera. Building an atmosphere of trust, mutual respect and camaraderie is initiated with these pre-interviews and must continue throughout the project. Those going on camera, especially non-managerial employees, must be convinced they have an element of control and will not be exploited.

Preliminary Documents

When research is completed, the writer should produce the documents that follow initial research for any project: objectives, audience profile, content outline and treatment. In addition, the writer should also describe the rationale for producing in a documentary mode. The excerpt below is from the writer's initial report on results of Quality Circle research, which included pre-interviews with several potential on-camera participants.

> *Assumption*: Extracorporeal's experiences implementing the Quality Circle concept in Tampa are ideally suited to treatment as a television documentary.

> *Rationale*: To fully appreciate the Quality Circle concept, one must experience the group dynamics of a Quality Circle in action. The problem solving and communication that result are most compelling when *told directly by the people involved*.

> Documentary footage of actual Quality Circle sessions... interviews with management...employee demonstrations of specific quality and productivity improvements...such location footage could provide vivid insight into the inner workings of Quality Circles. The show-and-tell style of the television documentary offers a perfect format for this type of material.

> Location coverage documents the process and the results in a highly credible, believable manner. After all, an employee's enthusiastic identification with management goals is the very essence of your story. What better way to capture that personal commitment than through the personal medium of television?

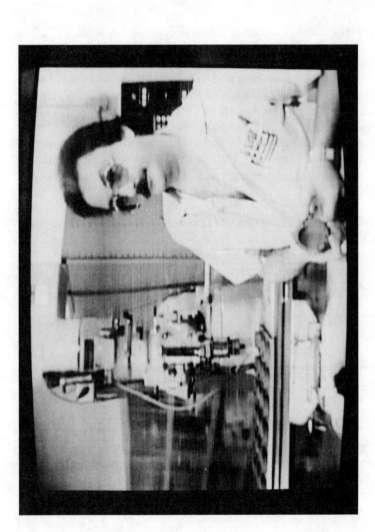

Interview subjects often find it easier to talk candidly in their work surroundings. Courtesy Johnson and Johnson.

The writer's recommendation obviously stems from firsthand discussions with those individuals who will participate on camera. Knowledge of the participants and the viewpoints they are able to express on camera is vital to developing detailed pre-production planning documents.

The Treatment

In contrast to scripted formats, where the treatment simply functions as a preliminary checkpoint prior to a first draft script, the treatment for an unscripted program serves as the basis for the client's approval to proceed with production. Based on research and pre-production interviews, the writer's vision of the finished program should include a sense of how various interview comments will be interwoven to communicate content. To illustrate, look at these excerpts from the Quality Circle treatment. (Although this material is taken from an actual project, fictional names are used here.)

> ...The scene shifts to the General Manager's area, where we see Jim Kilgore interacting with office staff members. Narration sets the stage for interview comments: "Jim Kilgore describes the situation at Extracorporeal when he became the plant's new General Manager in 1979..."
>
> Cut to interview footage of Kilgore describing "inherited" problems: order backlogs, rework, absenteeism, etc.
>
> Narrator introduces Ben Robling, Quality Control Manager. In interview footage, he describes his first exposure to the Quality Circle concept. Intercut Robling comments with the Kilgore interview as they recount the initial factors and concerns which influenced their decision to start a Quality Circle. They refer to the role of an outside consultant, and we cut to interview footage of Dr. Richard Hess explaining the involvement of his firm. Rhythmic intercutting between Kilgore, Robling and Hess as they address major considerations and prerequisite training needed for Quality Circle start-up...
>
> Transition to describe group dynamics of Quality Circle interaction. Combine voice-over comments from Hess, Robling, and appropriate Quality Circle leaders with MOS shots [without sound; see Glossary] of Circles in action. Interview comments focus on mechanics of Quality Circle start-up and

operation, outlining approaches to problem identification, cause-effect analysis, brainstorming and recommendations to management...

Once the Quality Circle modus operandi has been established, focus shifts to exploration of specific case study examples of successful problem solving...A terse statement of the problem is voiced by the narrator...then, cut to interview footage showing an employee from the Quality Circle explaining how the Circle attacked the problem. . .

Notice the writer not only identifies who will appear on camera, but indicates when they will be introduced and how their comments will be interwoven. The narrator's bridging role is alluded to, as well as a sense of visual materials that will illustrate interview footage.

Content Outline

The treatment, however, is merely a broad-brush overview. Details on what the program will cover and which on-camera participants are expected to make each point are spelled out in the content outline. In developing a content outline for an unscripted program, I prefer a page layout which correlates content points, interview questions and on-camera participants at a glance, as in Figure 9.1. (It's usually easiest to lay out the format horizontally.) Since interview footage of real people provides the source of major content points, this layout clearly links content to specific interviews and shows the extent of each participant's involvement. From this, the writer and the producer/director can evaluate whether the people selected for interviewing are appropriate. Should there be more or fewer interviews? Is there an appropriate mix of individuals to ensure a balanced perspective?

Interview Sheets

Next, the writer develops individual interview sheets, listing specific questions for each person scheduled to appear on camera. Much of this work is already down on paper, since the content outline includes a core list of questions directed toward each person. In the content outline, however, questions are organized by content points, not individuals. The interview sheet is worked up by extracting all questions which pertain to a single individual.

If, for example, we list on a separate piece of paper all questions

Figure 9.1: Content Outline for an Unscripted Program

CONTENT POINTS	QUESTIONS	WHO RESPONDS
I. Introduction to Quality Circle concept.	How did you first learn about Quality Circles? What research did you do? What made you think the concept would work at Extracorporeal?	J. Kilgore B. Robling
II. Corporate management's viewpoint.	What was your initial opinion of the Quality Circle concept for the Tampa Plant? How important is top management support to implementing Quality Circles?	B. Elliot D. Whitson
III. "Selling" the Quality Circle concept to middle management and supervisors.	How did you go about introducing this concept to plant management? What was the initial reaction? What groundwork was done to pave the way for a positive response? (For Consultant) How typical was the initial response at Extracorporeal?	J. Kilgore B. Robling T. Sparks R. Hess
IV. Issue—middle management/supervisor's resistance to Quality Circle concept.	What was your initial reaction to the idea of Quality Circles here? What were your "worst fears?" Did they materialize? Why or why not? How much actual problem solving did you think would come from Quality Circles?	T. Sparks H. Nason G. Brown S. Harris R. Burbick R. Wallach

Figure 9.1: Content Outline for an Unscripted Program (cont.)

CONTENT POINTS	QUESTIONS	WHO RESPONDS
	Have you had to alter your management style to accomodate the Quality Circle concept?	
V. Quality Circles in action		
A. Definition	Just what is a Quality Circle?	R. Hess
		B. Robling
	Why is a Circle composed of people doing similar work?	
	Why is the size of a Circle important?	
B. Method of operation	How often do they meet?	R. Hess
		B. Robling
	What distinguishes a Quality Circle from a general "bull session?"	
	What is the rationale behind the frequency and the length of meetings?	
C. Techniques involved in running a Quality Circle.	How does a team identify problems?	B. Robling
		R. Hess
	How do they select what problems to work on?	Selected circle leaders
		Actuality footage from circle meetings
	How do they gather data?	
	What do they do with the data collected?	
	How are suggestions for solving problems evaluated?	
	How are results reported to management?	

appearing by the name B. Robling, we have the beginnings of an
interviewer's set of questions. Usually, the writer finds those questions
need reordering for a more cohesive interview. Also, additional questions,
particularly introductory warm-ups or icebreakers, as well as potential
follow-up probes, may be added. Check to see that all interview questions
are left open-ended so they elicit substantive comments, observations and
analytical remarks. A string of yes and no answers is death to any
interview.

A sample interview sheet for B. Robling is shown in Figure 9.2. Note the
use of introductory warm-ups and potential follow-ups to supplement core
questions. A list of individual interview questions should be devised for
each person or each group of individuals. If you'll be asking essentially the
same questions of several different supervisors, for instance, then it's
probably only necessary to develop a generic Supervisor's Interview Sheet.

The value of all these individual planning documents is that, even
though the program is unscripted, those involved in the production have a
clear sense of what will need to happen to obtain the footage to tell the
story. This is especially important if the writer is not involved in shooting.
The treatment provides an overall description of the ultimate viewing
experience. The content outline shows how interview questions will yield
the substantive comments to cover the subject. Interview sheets provide a
framework and plan of attack for each individual's participation. These
working documents can be cross-referenced and annotated during

Figure 9.2: Interview Sheet for Unscripted Format

PROJECT: Quality Circle Television Presentation   REEL #_____
INTERVIEW: Mr. Ben Robling

Questions   **Production Notes**

1) [Warm-up only.] Tell me about your personal
   background in the field of Quality Control
   management.

2) How would you assess the plant's performance prior
   to initiating Quality Circles? What were its strengths
   and weaknesses?

3) How did you first learn about Quality Circles?

Figure 9.2: Interview Sheet for Unscripted Format (cont.)

4) What research did you do?

5) What other quality improvement programs or measures did you consider?

6) How did you go about introducing this concept to plant management?

7) What was the initial reaction?

8) What groundwork was done to pave the way for a positive response?

9) Just what is a Quality Circle?

10) Why is a Circle composed of people doing similar work?

11) Why is the size of a Circle important?

12) How often do they meet?

13) What distinguishes a Quality Circle from a general "bull session"?

14) What is the rationale behind the frequency and length of the meetings?

15) How does a team identify problems?

16) How do they gather data?

17) What do they do with the data collected?

18) How are suggestions for solving problems evaluated?

19) How are results reported to management?

production to ensure that spontaneous, candid interviews are resulting in useful footage that can be integrated into the finished program. Though not a word of narration is yet involved, the writer's conceptual framework guides the entire production effort. When it comes time to fashion an edited program, large chunks of material should literally fall into place.

PRODUCTION

A writer's involvement in the actual production can vary. On some projects, the writer may simply observe interviews in progress, offering objective comment on their effectiveness. Sometimes it's appropriate for the writer to perform the interviewer's function. Theoretically, it's also possible for the writer to bow out at this stage and rejoin the staff after all the footage is in the can. Whatever the writer's role while shooting, there are certain principles in producing unscripted material to which writers should be sensitive in the program development phase.

Ask Good Questions and You'll Get Good Answers

This is simply a constructive way of saying "Don't put words in people's mouths." The reason for soliciting interviews in the first place is to capture the individual's personal observations. If the interviewer asks good questions, it results, in most cases, in good answers. Absurd as it may sound, I've seen corporate producers *script* answers for people about to be interviewed. That print-oriented mentality always results in a stilted, unconvincing and uninvolving viewing experience. A more common problem, however, is the subject who stays up all night scripting his own answers to anticipated questions. The result usually parallels the former problem: stilted, unconvincing and uninvolving.

It all goes back to trust. Each individual has been asked to participate on camera because he or she has viewpoints and experiences that help tell the full story. To convey that information credibly, participants simply need to converse with the interviewer. The director, the production crew, the interviewer—all are there to create an environment that instills confidence in the interviewee.

Stage for the Subject's Comfort

A non-threatening, relaxed environment is most conducive to a successful interview. Normally, this means conducting the session on the subject's own turf. Camera angles and lighting should be set so the subject and interviewer can make good eye contact, hear one another (an important consideration in factories or computer rooms) and be comfortable. Generally, people are most at ease at their own office or work area. However, if people work in an open office and the topic involves subjective, personal responses, a gaggle of gawking co-workers may inhibit the subject. In this case, a private office or secluded cafeteria area during off-hours might be more conducive. This is another reason for the writer's early involvement and the use of pre-production interview sessions. The writer can gain a sense of physical environments that are involved and suggest appropriate areas for each interview. Keep the psychological dynamics of the situation in mind when structuring unscripted formats.

Permit Interviews to Take on Their Own Life

Planning should generate the sense of direction and confidence necessary to allow the documentary style production to take on a life all its own. Interviewers should not follow the pre-ordained interview sheets slavishly. Optimally, the interview will take on the characteristics of a two-way conversation. It will be a spontaneous and lively exchange; not a carbon copy of the original pre-interview. The interviewer should listen to the answers intently and ask follow-up questions as appropriate. There's always a list of prepared questions to fall back on. But the gems, the candid, utterly believable responses that make for the most compelling on-screen comments, generally spring not from pat interview questions but from the animated give and take of two individuals discussing a subject in depth.

Subjects should also know that with video tape comments can be taped over, several times if necessary. Answers from various takes can be juxtaposed to make up the edited program. If proper technical arrangements are made, the interview can be played back on the spot. There's plenty of opportunity to retake the entire interview or selected portions as often as necessary. (All these provisions help build trust.)

Whether the writer acts as interviewer or participates by watching each interview with a critical eye for how well responses can be integrated into the overall structure, it's important to make continual reference to the production planning documents during taping. At the end of each take, jot down responses you find particularly good in the appropriate area of the content outline. Then, halfway through production, when the producer or the director wants to know what content areas need to be explored in more depth, someone has a handle on where the holes or thin spots are. In either case, the writer plays an active role in the production process—and is mentally already working on the post-production phase.

POST-PRODUCTION

Review Footage

The first step in turning individual interviews into a cohesive television presentation is to review interviews in their entirety. If feasible, it's helpful to have transcripts of the interviews at the same time. One experienced producer of corporate unscripted programs has audio cassettes made of each day's video taping. Those audio cassettes are then sent out for transcription. Shortly after shooting, writer, producer and director all have a complete set of transcripts to work with. Even with transcripts, however, screening of footage is mandatory. Words on paper will not accurately convey the potential of actual footage. Vocal inflection, pacing, gesture, facial expression, even the camera angle may add or detract from a specific comment's usefulness.

In the first review, look for how interview comments play on the screen. If you have a transcript, follow along, making notes to indicate usable comments. If transcripts have not been made, jot down notes and video cassette counter numbers of those interview segments that appear most usable.

Once you have an overall sense of the material available to work with, begin to attack it from an organizational standpoint. Five-by-eight file cards can be quite useful for this preliminary organization. Write down the speaker's name and the general topic, and include the verbatim quote or the in and out cues (the opening and closing words of the quote). The file card should also contain references to help the physical editing process. The sample card in Figure 9.3 includes the video cassette player count number (**1**), which makes it easy to locate the segment on the cassette. At the same time, if the cassette copy includes the SMPTE time code display, make a notation of in and out time codes on the file card (**2**). The Society of Motion Picture and Television Engineers (SMPTE) electronic time code indicates a specific frame by giving the reel number and the elapsed time on the tape by minutes, seconds and frame number. (There are 30 frames per second.) Both editor and director will refer to these codes when editing the video tape. The In Cue time code corresponds to the first frame of usable video; the Out Cue to the last frame from the excerpt. The time noted in the lower right hand corner (**3**) of the card is the running time or duration of the specific interview comment—26 seconds in this case.

**Figure 9.3: File Card of Interview Comments
for an Unscripted Format**

JIM KILGORE	TOPIC: Initial Reactions	Reel #: *17*
Cassette **(1)**		*Time Code* **(2)**
153	IN: "The initial reaction of the managers, I think..."	17:06:16:25
	OUT: "...not going to probably work."	17:06:42:05
		(3) :26

Develop Continuity

Once you have all relevant interview comments on a given topic logged on file cards, you can identify the people who will carry the freight through their comments and begin to rough out major program segments. The cards are extremely functional for this task. They can be arranged and rearranged in various sequences to see how well certain comments dovetail and play in juxtaposition. One of the first problems the writer usually encounters is redundancy, several people saying essentially the same thing. Eliminate these redundancies by selecting the strongest statements. Discard those that may lack clarity or believability. Look for the most succinct expressions of an idea; they are generally strongest.

When you find a sequence of comments that covers a given topic with clarity and is likely to play well on screen, the program segment can be transferred from file cards to edit log sheets. Figure 9.4 shows one edit log format which is particularly suited to plotting out unscripted material. These edit log pages are extremely useful, not only to the writer, but to the director and video tape editor as well. First, each page is identified at the

Figure 9.4: Edit Log Sheet for an Unscripted Format

EDIT LOGS—Quality Circles

TOPIC: Initial Reactions

SPEAKER	CASSETTE	IN CUE:	OUT CUE:	TIME CODE	DURATION
J. Kilgore R17	153	"The initial reaction of the managers, I think...	...not going to probably work."	17:06:16:25 17:06:42:05	:26
S. Harris R4	461	"I guess basically, in the back of everybody's mind...	...do your job better than you were doing."	04:24:02:05 04:24:16:17	:14
J. Kilgore R17	163	"I think the initial reaction from the supervisors was that they...	...and that they would lose control on the floor."	17:06:44:01 17:07:01:03	:15
R. Wallach R7	493	"I think the statement I'll have to make. . .	...the product that actually pays the bills."	07:26:28:18 07:26:58:10	:30
J. Kilgore R17	170	"I would think that the first concern from the engineers...	...from the people on the floor on a timely basis?"	17:07:02:23 17:07:20:18	:18
G. Brown R2	661	"There's always a bit of egotism on the part of engineers...	...does have a better way to do it."	02:39:46:02 02:40:21:21	:35

2:18

top by the general topic being discussed; in this case, initial reactions. These topics headings correspond with main points of the original content outline.

Next, a series of columns provides all information necessary for an editor to physically cut the sequence together on video tape. Column 1 identifies the speaker and the video tape production reel from which the scene is taken. Column 2 gives a video cassette counter reference. Columns 3 and 4 provide a verbatim transcription of the opening and closing words for each specific statement. And Column 5 gives the SMPTE time code number. With both content cues and time code numbers, any editor should be able to piece the sequence together whether familiar with the material or not. Column 6 contains the running time or duration of that specific excerpt. At the bottom, the column is totalled to provide the running time for the complete sequence.

This obsession with time in an unscripted format is important for two reasons. First, the length of individual comments and the sequence in which they're juxtaposed establishes the pace of the program. Secondly, the screen time given over to various topics says a good deal about the relative importance placed on each.

Scripting Narration

Once the skeleton of the program is on paper, the writer can focus on fleshing it out with the narrative copy. If the writer has been involved in the project from the research phase on, the narrative wrap-arounds should fall into place easily. The narrator's role has been established in the treatment. With intimate knowledge of the interview content available for each segment, the writer should have copy points and style already in mind.

Generally, narration fulfills three distinct functions in such programming. As an introduction, the copy establishes main themes and content areas as a lead-in to interview footage. Short transitional bridges are usually necessary to link closely related sequences of interview comments. Finally, narration may also be used to convey factual material, condensations of complex interview responses or other content that is illuminating but not functional or economical to convey in interviews.

Since the writer knows the specific actuality cues that will surround a narrative segment, the narration can be written to segue naturally into interview footage. The writer should also have visual footage in mind as cutaway material to cover narrative links. This may range from shots of the on-camera participants in daily situations to detailed graphics or action footage. The following lead-in to the subject "Initial Reactions" to Quality Circles at Extracorporeal indicates specific cutaway footage. In addition, the narrator's copy provides a natural bridge to the first interview statement.

VIDEO	AUDIO
Continue MOS footage of Robling and other production workers—highlight footage which shows interaction between management and production worker.	**OFF-CAMERA NARRATOR**: THE NOTION THAT HOURLY EMPLOYEES CAN BEST IDENTIFY AND SOLVE CERTAIN PRODUCTION PROBLEMS IS NEW TO MANY AMERICAN MANAGERS AND SUPERVISORS. THE INITIAL REACTIONS AT EXTRACORPOREAL'S TAMPA PLANT ARE QUITE TYPICAL:
Carry MOS footage featuring Jim Kilgore through a portion of the opening interview statement.	ACTUALITY INSERT: Topic—Initial Reactions

The Rough Cut

Once all narrated segments are scripted, the entire program exists on paper for the first time. Although an edited master could be made by simply following cues on paper, usually there is need for an interim step: a rough cut version of the program, which serves several functions. It allows the writer and the director to see how specific scenes play as a viewing experience. Almost invariably, both writer and director see things they want to change: a particular comment is confusing out of context; a segment bogs down in a lengthy anecdote, which, though interesting, dulls the narrative thrust.

Additionally, the rough cut gives the producer a vehicle for testing the program with the client or content experts, with management and, if appropriate, even with sample members of the target audience. Comments and reactions from such people are extremely valuable in arriving at final editorial decisions. By this point in the project, writer, producer, director and perhaps even client are too close to the material to be completely objective. Fresh eyes and ears will be quick to sense when the program drags or that a particular statement lacks clarity or that the relative time devoted to a content point seems excessive.

For such input to be constructive, the writer and the producer/director should not be defensive about criticism. You're seeking people's honest reactions to a work in progress, so don't short-circuit the process by resisting suggestions. Hear each person out; then analyze the input you receive objectively and dispassionately. Ultimately, you must trust your own judgment and taste. But every writer needs an editor, and, in an unscripted production, the rough cut is the best tool available for soliciting such input.

CONCLUSION: STRIVE FOR BALANCE

The key to successfully producing in the unscripted mode is to strike a balance, consciously controlling through planning yet simultaneously allowing the project to take on a life of its own. Ideally, the final product will be marked by an air of spontaneity that translates into a high degree of believability, while covering essential content points concisely and in an organized fashion.

The writer can contribute a great deal to the effort, not so much as a wordsmith but as a conceptual thinker, planner and organizer of content. This can prove as satisfying as seeing thirty pages of original narration translated into a viewing experience. But the writer needs to understand and accept that, by and large, an unscripted program will be *written* by those interviewed for the project.

10

Writing The Nonbroadcast Drama

*   *   *

A middle-aged executive reaches out and slaps his jangling alarm clock, then pads groggily to the bathroom. Under the pulsating hot water, consciousness slowly sets in: "Simply must go easier on the martinis tonight. Or maybe it's the vino with dinner that produces such an anesthetized head."

He does the customary "fast forward" preview of his day. "Have to finish that memo on the train. Then there's the Thursday staff meeting at ten. Lunch with the visiting scientists from the Land of the Rising Sun. . .The afternoon's still open. . ." He faces up to an unpleasant task: "I'll have to make sure and get Robertson on tap for this afternoon. The man's a complete bafflement. . .A year ago his group was blazing the way, solving design problems faster than we could assign them. But this year—a total reversal. His group's months behind in debugging the hydraulics, and that's delaying the entire project. Progress reports come in later and later. And why does he refuse to fire Singleton when a year ago he wrote a memo justifying why the guy should be out on the street. . .I just must have a very serious talk with Mr. Robertson. He's too valuable a group leader to see go down the tubes like this. . ."

Across town, Bill Robertson is also getting ready for work—sharing the bathroom with his school-teaching wife. "You sure you're not making an emotional decision?" his wife asks.

"Of course it's an emotional decision! I can't stand working in that place another day. . .I've been stewing over it for months now. But it's finally clear to me that they put Dickerson into my group to train him as my replacement. Since he came, it simply hasn't been the same. The group's gone to hell. And there's not a thing I can do about it. They want me outta there anyway—so I'm just doing them a favor—ouch!" Bill cuts himself shaving just as their kindergarten-age daughter calls from the foot of the stairs: "The water's boiling over, Mommy."

Now it's two o'clock, and Bill Robertson is ushered into his boss's office. They greet one another with steady determination. There's tension in the handshake itself. . .

*   *   *

Imagine the dramatic potential of the scene that's about to unfold. Successfully bringing the scene to life, however, will require writing skills quite different from those we've explored to this point. In this chapter, we'll look at the nonbroadcast writer as dramatist and examine the usefulness of dramatic forms and character-voice narrations for nonbroadcast subjects.

NONBROADCAST DRAMATIC APPLICATIONS

The worlds of college campus, corporate headquarters, and medical center are rife with wonderful dramatic situations. Dramatizing such interpersonal relationships is a useful way to depict human behavior in a form that permits objective analysis. Dramatic vignettes serve as case studies or role models for such interpersonal skills as interviewing job applicants, employee supervision and counseling, even dealing with an irate customer. Video dramatizations can be a graphic teaching aid when developing these human relations skills in the classroom.

But the usefulness of dramatizations for the nonbroadcast writer is not limited to personal interactions. Dramatizations have proven a surprisingly effective way of breathing life into key points of anti-trust law, of illustrating the treatment of a heart attack victim, even explaining the inner workings of a new computer system. And, in addition to full-fledged dramas, many presentations make use of character-voice narrators. A fictional character, whether played by a live actor or depicted through artwork, puppets or animation, allows the writer to present content with an editorial slant not usually possible through a factual, objective narrative style.

With such obvious potential, one might ask why so many nonbroadcast vignettes appear wooden and contrived and fail to offer a convincing portrayal of reality. Many factors contribute. Some, such as amateurish acting and directing, may be beyond the writer's control. But just as often the writer fails to give the performers and the director realistic characters and dialog to work with. Take this vignette, for instance.

Fictional characters give the writer flexibility to convey messages with an imagination and flair that are often impossible with a corporate spokesperson. In "The Personal Side of Selling," puppets convey tips on proper grooming and attitude for sales representative in a whimsical, lighthearted manner. Copyright 1982, The Prudential Insurance Company of America. Reprinted by permission. Available through Insurance Learning Systems, Inc.

"Cardboard Character" Dialog

ROGER: PLEASE, COME IN, CAROL. HAVE A SEAT. CAN I GET YOU SOME COFFEE?

CAROL: NO THANK YOU, ROGER, NOT RIGHT NOW.

ROGER: CAROL, I HAVE BEEN
MEANING TO GET TOGETHER WITH
YOU FOR SOME TIME NOW TO
DISCUSS THE SERIOUS PROBLEMS
WE ARE EXPERIENCING ON THE
ANDERSON ACCOUNT. . .

CAROL: YES—I EXPECTED AS MUCH.
I FIGURED THAT'S WHY YOU
WANTED TO SEE ME.

ROGER: CAROL, WHAT WENT
WRONG? HOW CAN WE BE ON THE
BRINK OF LOSING THE ENTIRE
ACCOUNT WITH ALMOST NO
WARNING?

CAROL: I DON'T KNOW, ROGER. I
HAVE BEEN TRYING TO FIGURE
THAT OUT MYSELF FOR WEEKS
NOW. . .

Character, Conflict and Content

Several things mar this short exchange. Granted, the dialog could be
made more naturally conversational. But there are more deep-seated
problems symptomatic of writers who have not taken the steps necessary
to create characters and construct dramatic scenes which play realistically
on camera. The excerpt above lacks the two classic ingredients of any
dramatic situation: character and conflict.

Good dramatizations are more than a succession of individual speeches.
Scripting dramatic action places a special demand on the writer to develop
interaction between two or more *characters*. The writer must create imaginary people so life-like that the viewer accepts them as real. To do this, you
must know your characters as well as you know family and friends—how
they think, feel and behave, and how they respond to others in varying
situations.

The second requirement of a dramatic situation goes back to the ancient
Greek theater: conflict. Characters pursuing contradictory goals are the
heart of rich dramatic situations. This doesn't mean a simple employment
interview will match the ravings of Oedipus, although there is plenty of
dramatic tension inherent in any encounter between prospective employee
and employer. Often, dramatic conflict springs from commonplace, daily

happenings. Look at the characterizations and relationships in any number of successful network television sitcoms involving ordinary men and women in daily situations. Episodes are rich in dramatic potential not because of what happens (plot), but because of the interaction between the human beings involved (characterization).

The nonbroadcast dramatic format, however, places additional burdens on the scriptwriter. Most nonbroadcast dramatic vignettes must not only play as drama but simultaneously fulfill specific communication or training objectives and be geared to the specific viewing audience. Dramatic action must be totally functional, illustrating key content points about the workings of a computer system, for instance, or the intricacies of a complex insurance policy. Quite often, the dramatic vignette will not stand alone but be part of a larger instructional curriculum. Thus, the flexibility to develop characters and establish relationships is often constrained, and the nonbroadcast dramatist must develop a crisp, economical dramatic style.

This chapter offers techniques that will help with this special form. Dramatic writing, however, remains a discipline with its own unique requirements. The skills necessary to succeed with this format are rooted in the theater. Theatrical experience or training will be a big asset to any writer facing this type of assignment.

CHARACTERIZATION

Characterization has two components: internal attributes and external manifestations of those attributes. Internal attributes are inherent characteristics and traits associated with an individual's personality, which can usually be described with single adjectives or short phrases to profile the character. For instance, look at the following listing of attributes for two imaginary characters. Both are high achievers and successful in their careers.

Internal Attributes Character A	Internal Attributes Character B
Ambitious	Ambitious
Hard-driving, aggressive	Friendly, outgoing
Arrogant	Highly knowledgeable
Impatient	Even-tempered
Distrusts colleagues and subordinates	A team player
Likes to make all the decisions	Willing to delegate responsibility

Even though these lists of attributes suggest two distinctly different personalities, they remain generalized descriptions of *internal* qualities. To create a flesh-and-blood character, the dramatist must illustrate internal attributes through the character's external words, actions and behavior. To bring characters to life through their external manifestations, it's often helpful to list a character's internal attributes in one column, then the specific ways in which those attributes will be manifested in another column, as in the following example for Character A.

Character A

Internal Attributes	External Manifestations
Ambitious	Overly solicitous and courteous with superiors
Hard-driving, aggressive	Seems to do several things at once Barks orders Speaks and moves rapidly
Impatient	Chain smokes Cuts people off in mid-sentence
Arrogant	Never thanks secretary
Distrusts colleagues and subordinates	Second-guesses subordinate's decision
Likes to make all the decisions	Refuses to allow subordinate to make important business trip alone; must accompany subordinate

Of course, not all of a character's attributes will be manifested externally at once—a scene might be devoted exclusively to illustrating one trait. Other traits and manifestations, however, could be combined and illustrated in a single scene. The important point, at this stage, is to recognize that the nonbroadcast dramatist must define and develop character in order to arrive at convincing dramatizations.

CONFLICT

Notice that the arrogant boss's external manifestations are shown through interaction with other characters: superiors, subordinates and secretary. In a dramatic format, interaction between characters serves as the mechanism for character development. In this case, each interaction will provide opportunities for the character to show internal traits—from acting overly solicitous with superiors to barking orders to subordinates—and each could form the nucleus for a dramatic scene. Until now, we have discussed scenes in the sense of television script organization. In a dramatic context, however, a scene takes on additional connotations and can be classified according to the *function* it performs in communicating content.

- Expository scenes introduce characters and convey information to the audience.

- Transitional scenes move the action in time, place or context.

- Development scenes probe and explore character or situation in detail.

- Climactic scenes present the culmination of character development and conflict.

The writer consciously structures each scene to achieve an intended effect. Each separate interaction between characters serves a purpose: to illuminate character, to convey information, and to advance the plot. Often, a single scene serves several purposes simultaneously.

In classical dramatic structure, scenes are arranged to build toward the climactic moment—the point at which characters' conflicting motivations are at their peak. A brief denouement usually follows to resolve the conflict. Such a classical form may not always suit the communicative or instructional needs of the nonbroadcast dramatist. However, realistic dramatizations must contain elements of tension, conflicting emotions and characters working at cross-purposes in order to involve the viewer and arouse interest in what happens next.

Think back to the sample dialog between Roger and Carol. It fails to make the viewer care because the characters themselves seem detached, uninvolved emotionally. In the face of a serious problem, Carol is far too amenable. More legitimate reactions from her in such a situation could range from a guarded foreboding of an unpleasant confrontation to actually breaking down and sobbing. From the dramatist's point of view, tears would make Roger's counseling session that much more of an ordeal.

Even Roger's dialog is too pat and straightforward for a man about to embark on a delicate counseling session.

One aid to the writer in developing tension and conflict is to define each character in terms of his or her *motivation* at any given moment. To put it another way, you should know what each character wants from the interaction. Take a look at this excerpt from an EEO training program, an expository scene that establishes one step in the evolution of a major communication breakdown.[1]

Excerpt 1 from "Equal Employment Opportunity"

> GLENDA: I THINK IF WE REORGANIZED THE DEPARTMENT ALONG THOSE LINES, WE'D FIND THAT WE COULD IMPLEMENT WITH A LOT FEWER PROBLEMS. YOU KNOW WHAT A HASSLE IT IS WHEN THE FIELD HAS TO HELP US DEBUG A SYSTEM.
>
> HANK: I'VE GOT TO ADMIT—IT LOOKS SOUND ON PAPER, GLENDA. LET ME DIGEST ALL THIS AND WE'LL TRY AND DETERMINE WHAT THE NEXT STEP SHOULD BE.
>
> GLENDA: GOOD. WELL, I'D BETTER GET BACK TO THE MORE MUNDANE STUFF. (Gets up to leave.)
>
> HANK: JUST OUT OF CURIOSITY— HOW ARE WE COMING ON ALL THE MUNDANE STUFF?
>
> GLENDA: IT'S GETTING THERE— BUT. . .

---

[1] From "Equal Employment Opportunity," written and produced by William Van Nostran, directed by James G. Libby. Copyright Crum & Forster Corporation, 1982. Used by permission.

HANK: BUT WHAT?

GLENDA: THERE'S A LOT GOING ON OUT THERE. YOU KNOW THAT.

HANK: HOW ABOUT THE NEW CLAIMS RECORD SYSTEM FOR THE SOUTHERN REGION?

GLENDA: I'M AFRAID WE'VE RUN INTO SOME PROBLEMS ON IT, HANK.

HANK: PROBLEMS? WHAT KIND OF PROBLEMS?

GLENDA: NOTHING I CAN'T STRAIGHTEN OUT. (Uncertain, tentative.) IT'S JUST GOING TO TAKE SOME TIME. AND NEXT WEEK I'M GOING TO LOSE HARRY FOR A WEEK'S VACATION. HE'S A KEY MAN ON THE PROJECT—BUT I'VE HAD HIM SCRUB VACATION ONCE ALREADY. THE BIG PROBLEM'S TIME. . .

HANK: WELL, YOU'RE IN CHARGE OUT THERE. IF YOU TELL ME YOU'LL GET IT ALL STRAIGHTENED OUT, THEN I'VE GOTTA GO WITH YOU. . .

In this scene, Glenda, a newly promoted supervisor, is motivated by a desire to keep her boss from thinking the problems she faces are beyond her ability to solve. Hank, on the other hand, wants to show his support by an expression of confidence in Glenda's abilities. The scene establishes a lack of candor and frankness on both parties. Other scenes continue this pattern of behavior, culminating in a climactic scene of outright conflict.

Excerpt 2 from "Equal Employment Opportunity"

HANK: GLENDA, COME ON IN. DO YOU HAVE A FEW MINUTES?

GLENDA: YEAH, HANK. A FEW. WE'VE GOT A LOT GOING ON. PRIORITIES, YOU KNOW.

HANK: I PROMISE NOT TO TAKE UP TOO MUCH TIME. I JUST WANT TO MAKE SURE EVERYTHING'S SET FOR IMPLEMENTING THE NEW CLAIMS RECORD SYSTEM FOR THE SOUTHERN REGION TUESDAY.

GLENDA: TUESDAY? C'MON, HANK, BE REALISTIC.

HANK: GLENDA, WHAT ARE YOU TALKING ABOUT? YOU'VE KNOWN FOR SIX WEEKS THE DEADLINE FOR IMPLEMENTING THAT PROGRAM WAS THE 16TH. YOU'RE NOT TELLING ME IT'S NOT READY, ARE YOU?

GLENDA: HANK, THERE'S A LOT GOING ON RIGHT NOW. BELIEVE ME—WE'RE MOVING AS FAST AS HUMANLY POSSIBLE.

HANK: I CAN'T BELIEVE WHAT I'M HEARING. DIDN'T WE JUST HAVE A BIG SESSION ABOUT ESTABLISHING PRIORITIES AND STICKING TO THEM?

GLENDA: WELL, YES. . .WE DID.

HANK: AND WASN'T THAT YOUR BIG GRIPE? THAT WE'D GET MORE ACCOMPLISHED IF WE SET PRIORITIES AND STUCK TO THEM?

GLENDA: YES, HANK. IT WAS MY SOAP BOX. THERE'S JUST ONE

THING YOU KEEP OVERLOOKING
THOUGH.

HANK: YEAH. AND WHAT MIGHT
THAT BE?

GLENDA (Exasperated.) EVERYTHING
CAN'T BE A PRIORITY, HANK. IF
EVERY PROJECT'S A PRIORITY—
THEN NO PROJECT'S A PRIORITY!

HANK: (Deliberately.) YOU WANNA
KNOW WHAT I THINK THE PROBLEM
IS GLENDA? THE REAL PROBLEM?

GLENDA: THE PROBLEM IS THAT
WITH FOUR IMPLEMENTATIONS
THIS MONTH—ONE OF 'EM'S GOING
TO HAVE TO SLIP. . .

HANK: GLENDA, WHEN I GAVE YOU
THIS PROMOTION, I HAD NO
DOUBTS ABOUT YOUR TECHNICAL
ABILITY. NONE WHATSOEVER.
YOU'RE HEAD AND SHOULDERS
ABOVE EVERYONE OUT ON THAT
FLOOR. BUT I TOLD YOU THEN, AND
I'M TELLING YOU NOW—
SOMETIMES YOU'VE GOT TO PUSH
PEOPLE TO THE LIMIT TO GET THE
WORK OUT. IT'S THAT SIMPLE.

GLENDA: HANK, WE'VE BEEN OVER
THIS BEFORE, AND IF I'M ANY MORE
DEMANDING THEY'RE GOING TO BE
CALLING ME THE DRAGON LADY!

HANK: WELL, IF YOU'RE SO
DEMANDING, HOW COME THIS
SYSTEM'S NOT READY FOR
IMPLEMENTATION?

GLENDA: I TOLD YOU WE WERE
FALLING BEHIND LAST WEEK!

HANK: YOU TOLD ME NOTHING OF
THE SORT. NOW TELL ME
STRAIGHT—EXACTLY HOW FAR
BEHIND ARE YOU? A COUPLE OF
DAYS? (Pause.) A WEEK?

GLENDA: AT LEAST—MAYBE TEN
DAYS.

HANK: GLENDA, IF YOU KNEW YOU
WERE GOING TO BE THIS FAR OFF
TARGET, YOU SHOULD'VE SAID
SOMETHING A LONG TIME AGO.

GLENDA: I WENT ON RECORD WITH
YOU LAST WEEK!

HANK: I'M SORRY, GLENDA—BUT
YOU NEVER SAID A WORD TO ME.

GLENDA: YOU'RE JUST NOT BEING
FAIR, HANK, AND YOU KNOW IT. I
THINK YOU JUST DON'T WANT TO
HEAR WHAT I'M TELLING YOU SO
YOU IGNORE IT. . .

In this scene, the motivations of each character *change* as the situation
unfolds. At first, Hank is motivated solely by a desire to be reassured that
all is well for the claims record system implementation. Later, he needs to
know the extent of the delay. Once the situation is clearly out of hand from
his view, his motivation shifts to placing blame on Glenda for lack of
toughness in dealing with her staff.

In developing dramatizations, then, scenes function as building blocks
that the writer uses to show the evolution of the relationship between two
or more characters. To ensure the characters are believable, the writer

must know their internal traits and have a strategy for revealing those traits through interaction with other characters. And, as we'll discuss later, dialog is the major means of revealing character and advancing plot.

DRAMATIC STYLE

Thus far, our focus has been on character development—a skill not required in more straightforward narrative formats. Additionally, there's the matter of dramatic style. Most dramatizations fall into one of two basic categories: realistic or presentational.

Realism in drama is often described as a treatment of character and action which resembles a slice of life. Unnoticed by the actors, the audience looks in on characters and situations that imitate real life as much as possible. There's a conscious effort on the part of writer, director, actors, scenic designers and other craftsmen to create this illusion of reality through dialog, characterization, action, settings and costume. The audience, for its part, accepts the premise of reality, willingly suspending disbelief and accepting actors and actresses as the flesh-and-blood characters they portray.

By direct contrast, in a presentational style, the dramatist, cast and crew often intentionally shatter the illusion of reality. The audience is frequently reminded they are watching a theatrical presentation as the actors periodically break character to speak directly to the audience. Other presentational techniques include highly stylized scenery, costumes or music. (In the theater, the integration of audio-visual material, such as film or slide projections, often characterizes this presentational style.) These effects are employed by playwrights as a way of catching the audience off guard and driving home didactic points.

Either of these two extremes in style could be successfully employed by the nonbroadcast television dramatist. After assessing audience, content and objectives, the writer should settle on the stylistic mode which best meets the needs of a given project.

To illustrate these two styles in the context of nonbroadcast programming, let's look at two different approaches to the same subject. Both were used in a program about sexual harassment on the job. Each involves dramatic action that focuses on a supervisor making sexual demands on an employee. The first is a realistic treatment of this situation.[2]

---

[2]From "Sexual Harassment: Fact or Fiction," written by William Van Nostran, directed by James G. Libby and produced by William J. Benham for AT&T Corporate Television. Used by permission.

Excerpt 1 from "Sexual Harassment: Fact or Fiction"

MS—On George and Cindy in George's office. George comes around from behind his desk to speak to Cindy seated in a chair.

GEORGE: CINDY, I JUST WANT YOU TO KNOW IN THE FEW MONTHS YOU'VE BEEN HERE—YOU'VE MADE A BIG IMPRESSION ON EVERYONE. ESPECIALLY YOURS TRULY.

CINDY: THANKS. . .I APPRECIATE IT, REALLY. I KNOW YOU'VE GIVEN ME A LOT OF EXTRA TIME AND HELP. . .

GEORGE: THAT'S ONLY BECAUSE I SEE YOU AS THE KIND OF PERFORMER WHO CAN BE PUT ON A FAST TRACK, YOU KNOW?

CINDY: THE JOB MEANS A LOT TO ME—THAT'S AWFULLY FLATTERING. . .

GEORGE: CINDY, I THINK WE KNOW ONE ANOTHER WELL ENOUGH THAT I CAN LEVEL WITH YOU. I THINK YOU AND I CAN HAVE A VERY PRODUCTIVE, LONG-TERM RELATIONSHIP. SO, WHY DON'T WE GET TO KNOW EACH OTHER BETTER. . .OFF THE JOB, THAT IS. WHY DON'T YOU MAKE PLANS TO HAVE DINNER WITH ME TOMORROW EVENING? WE'LL WRITE IT OFF AND CALL IT—A CAREER DEVELOPMENT SESSION. . .

CINDY: GEORGE. . .I HOPE YOU TAKE THIS IN THE SPIRIT IN WHICH IT'S INTENDED. I'M VERY HAPPY WITH

MY JOB...AND I LIKE THIS
DEPARTMENT A LOT...BUT, YOU'RE
MAKING ME MORE AND MORE
UNCOMFORTABLE...THOSE CARDS
YOU GIVE ME...THEY'RE
EMBARRASSING...AND I WISH YOU
WOULDN'T CONSTANTLY PUT YOUR
ARM AROUND ME...

GEORGE: (Off-balance.) CINDY, I
THINK YOU'VE GOT THE WRONG
IMPRESSION...

CINDY: (Keeps on rolling.) AND I WANT
TO DISCUSS CAREER
DEVELOPMENT...BUT I'D FEEL
BETTER ABOUT IT OVER LUNCH IN
THE CAFETERIA. WOULDN'T THAT
ACCOMPLISH THE SAME PURPOSE?

GEORGE: (He and Cindy continue on,
their audio pulled under.) I THINK
YOU'VE MADE YOUR POINT, CINDY.
AND IF I'VE OFFENDED YOU—YOU
CAN BE SURE IT WON'T HAPPEN
AGAIN...

The second scene which begins with a traditional narrative introduction, is presentational in style.

Excerpt 2 from "Sexual Harassment: Fact or Fiction"

TWO SHOT on both.   **FEMALE NARRATOR**: GOOD
REASONS TO TAKE THE ENTIRE
ISSUE OF SEXUAL HARASSMENT
SERIOUSLY. BUT THEN THE
QUESTION BECOMES: "WHAT
CONSTITUTES SEXUAL
HARASSMENT AT WORK?"

MALE NARRATOR: NOW WE'RE GETTING TO THE CRUX OF THE PROBLEM. SURE, THERE'S A TYPE OF BEHAVIOR WHICH IS BLATANT HARASSMENT. FOR INSTANCE, I CAN ENVISION THE SORT OF GUY WHO MIGHT. . .

FEMALE NARRATOR: THIS I WANT TO SEE!

MALE NARRATOR: OH, YOU NOT ONLY GET TO SEE IT, JENNIFER— YOU GET TO *LIVE* IT. . .

Special video effect, similar to transition to dream or other imagined event. It should be an obvious television "convention."

MUSIC & SOUND EFFX: (Theme and effects to clearly establish transition to fantasy sequence.)

Effect takes us through to scene set in office done in same "pop-up" art style.

ECU—On cover of Wall Street Journal. ZOOM out to reveal Male Narrator reading it at desk. His dress parodies the well-heeled executive: three-piece pin stripe suit; flower in lapel; gold cuff links and tie tack. He's also given a bit of grey at the

temples. Both
Narrators obviously
"play-act" these
scenes.

MALE NARRATOR: (To himself, after a groan.) WHY DO I ALWAYS LISTEN TO THAT IDIOT BROKER? (He puts the newspaper down in disgust. Then speaks through his intercom.) MISS PENNEYPINCH. . .

VOICE OF FEMALE NARRATOR: (Off camera.) YES, MR. LETCHWORTH?

MALE NARRATOR: (With a leer and unabashed lilt in his voice.) DICTATION TIME, MISS PENNEYPINCH!

MS—On entrance of
Female Narrator. She
is attired in a tight
fitting sweater dress;
giving her a buxom
appearance. She is
overly made up,
sports a blonde wig
and cracks chewing
gum. She plays this
scene as a cross
between Loni
Anderson and
Marilyn Monroe. She
moves to chair in
front of desk. . .

FEMALE NARRATOR: (Entering through doorway with steno pad.) IS THIS TO BE INTERCOMPANY CORRESPONDENCE OR A LETTER TO THE OUTSIDE WORLD?

MALE NARRATOR: THE DOOR, MISS PENNEYPINCH. . .I CAN'T CONCENTRATE WITH THE DOOR OPEN.

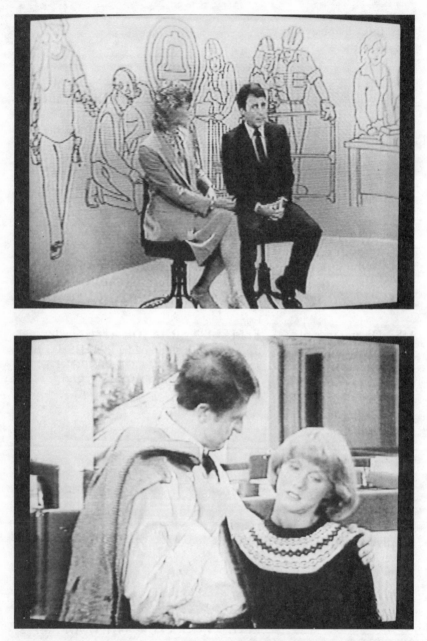

These four scenes from "Sexual Harassment: Fact or Fiction?"
illustrate blending of both presentational and "slice-of-life" styles.
The narrators are seen in a highly stylized studio environment.

Dramatic vignettes are taped on location for maximum reality. Transitions from studio commentary to location scenes are accomplished by matting location footage into a stylized flipchart.

FEMALE NARRATOR: BUT YOU
KNOW WE GET SO MUCH MORE
DONE WITH THE DOOR OPEN, MR.
LETCHWORTH. . .MAYBE JUST AJAR
A BIT?

MALE NARRATOR: (Fixated on her.)
MY DEAR, YOU'RE LOOKING TOO
GOOD TODAY TO EVEN THINK OF
LEAVING THE "JAR" "ADOOR". . .
(Realizing his flub.) UH. . .DOOR AJAR.
(He closes the door firmly. Then stalks
about her as he begins to dictate.) THIS
MEMO GOES TO R.O. HAMILTON. . .
SUBJECT: SEVERE INVENTORY
SHORTAGES. . .THE RECENT RASH
OF INVENTORY SHORTAGES,
COMMA. . .(He loses train of thought,
fixating on her again. She looks up.) READ
BACK WHAT YOU HAVE SO FAR. . .

Different angle—As
she reads, he leans
over her and places
arm around her. He's
obviously not listen-
ing.

FEMALE NARRATOR: TO: R.O.
HAMILTON. . .SUBJECT: SEVERE
INVENTORY SHORTAGES. . .THE
RECENT RASH OF INVENTORY
SHORTAGES, COMMA. . .

MALE NARRATOR: (Fondling her
shoulder.) MISS PENNEYPINCH, THAT
PERFUME. . .YOU KNOW WHAT IT
DOES TO ME? (He nuzzles.)

FEMALE NARRATOR: (To the audience,
breaking into her Narrator persona.)
JEEZ, WHAT A TRITE COME-ON. . .
(She rises, and refers to steno pad.) I
THINK YOU LEFT OFF IN THE
MIDDLE OF A SENTENCE, MR.
LETCHWORTH. . .

MALE NARRATOR: (Trying to compose himself.) I DID? OH YES. . .I WAS SAYING THAT YOUR PERFUME BRINGS OUT THE BEAST IN ME. . . (He pursues, she moves away, but it puts her in front of sofa.)

FEMALE NARRATOR: (Reading from pad.) YOU REALLY WANT MR. HAMILTON TO KNOW: "THE RECENT RASH OF INVENTORY SHORTAGES, COMMA, BRINGS OUT THE BEAST IN ME?

MALE NARRATOR: PUT THAT ASIDE. (Taking pad and pencil from her.) I'M TALKING ABOUT YOU AND ME, MISS PENNEYPINCH. WE CAN MAKE SUCH BEAUTIFUL MUSIC TOGETHER. (He leans into her, forcing her to plop onto the sofa.)

FEMALE NARRATOR: BUT WHAT ABOUT THE DUET YOU HAVE WITH—*MRS*. LETCHWORTH?

MALE NARRATOR: (He leans over her and kisses her neck.) COMPARED TO YOUR LOVELINESS, MRS. LETCHWORTH'S A WORN-OUT TUNE. . .AN OLD REFRAIN. . .

FEMALE NARRATOR: (To camera.) I JUST HOPE MOTHER NEVER SEES THIS. . .(She breaks free of him, rises, gathers her composure and emphatically says:) MR. LETCHWORTH! SHOULDN'T WE GET DOWN TO BUSINESS?

MALE NARRATOR: WELL PUT, MISS PENNEYPINCH. (With a sense of intimidation.) I HOPE YOU REALIZE YOUR CONTINUED EMPLOYMENT HERE DEPENDS ON *MY* PERSONAL ESTIMATE OF YOUR PER-FORMANCE?

FEMALE NARRATOR: (Intimidated.) YES, I'M WELL AWARE OF THAT, MR. LETCHWORTH.

MALE NARRATOR: GOOD. BECAUSE IF YOU'RE GOING TO PLAY IN MY ORCHESTRA—YOU'D BETTER PICK UP THE TEMPO!

FEMALE NARRATOR: MR. LETCHWORTH. . .I DON'T KNOW WHAT TO SAY. . .

MALE NARRATOR: ACTIONS SPEAK LOUDER THAN WORDS, MISS PENNEYPINCH. . . (He pursues with renewed vigor.)

Special video effect to highlight the trans-ition. . .

MUSIC AND SOUND EFFX: (Transitional theme to reality.)

DISSOLVE
THROUGH TO:

MS—On Narrators in studio setting, seated on stools in foreground. They are dressed as seen at the outset.

DIALOG THAT CONVEYS CONTENT

Whatever stylistic direction the writer chooses, dramatization is the narrative technique of telling a story through characters. Dialog between those characters becomes the primary vehicle for conveying information. In the theater, dialog and action combine to advance plot. In a nonbroadcast dramatization, plot per se is generally less significant. In most cases, the writer's task is to present either a role model of behavior (positive or negative) or to impart specific information through the dialog and action.

To accomplish this successfully, the writer must develop a facility for scripting dialog that is credible yet functional in conveying content. Unlike narration, which is conversational in style, but totally informational in function, dialog *is* a conversation. As such, dialog employs a definite give-and-take narrative structure and should have the rhythm and tempo of a tennis match. As the ball (dialog) is volleyed back and forth, each player (character) must react to the speed and direction of the opposing player's shot (line) in framing a return. As you read the script excerpts in this chapter, notice how this give-and-take rhythm makes the dialog appear to develop spontaneously, as each line prompts a reaction and, therefore, a related line from the other character. Notice too, that dialog is not necessarily a very *quick* way to convey information, but the forcefulness with which drama makes its points more than compensates.

In addition to the give-and-take structure, each character must speak in an idiom appropriate to his or her personality. Along with internal attributes and their external manifestations, a character's educational background, social standing and ethnic background should be reflected in speech and action. Read through the two scenes which follow. Though similar in action (one involves an employment interview; the other an employee counseling session), they differ in the socio-economic backgrounds of the characters. Notice how the tone of the dialog and idioms selected reflect the varying backgrounds and experiences of each character.[3]

---

[3]First excerpt: from "Equal Employment Opportunity Case Studies," written by William Van Nostran, directed by Daniel Klugherz, produced by Kenneth B. Wollny. © 1978 Mobil Oil Corporation. Reprinted by permission of Mobil Oil Corporation. Second excerpt: from "Employment Interviewing," written by William Van Nostran and Beverly Beach, directed by James G. Libby. Copyright Crum & Forster Corporation, 1982. Used by permission.

Excerpt from "Equal Employment Opportunity Case Studies"

BRAD ANDERSON: (Avoiding eye contact; not really relishing the situation he finds himself in.) SO TELL ME, JIM—AND I WANT YOU TO BE HONEST WITH US HERE—HOW D'YOU FEEL YOU'RE DOING RIGHT NOW? AS FAR AS THE JOB'S CONCERNED?

JIM RIVERS: WELL— BETTER. MUCH BETTER. I MEAN, I KNOW I MESSED UP THAT ONE ASSIGNMENT REAL BAD. BUT THAT WAS JUST NERVOUSNESS— FROM BEING NEW, YOU KNOW? I REALLY THINK I'M GETTING INTO THE GROOVE NOW. . .

BRAD: WELL, LOOK—I'M NOT OUT TO NAIL A PER-SON BECAUSE OF A SINGLE FOUL-UP. . .

JIM: I KNOW THAT, AND, WELL, I REALLY APPRE-CIATE YOUR SUPPORT. I MEAN, A LOTTA GUYS WOULD'VE HIT THE CEIL-ING WHEN THOSE PULLEYS WENT. I KNOW IT WAS A DUMB MISTAKE. BUT SOMETIMES THE HARDER YOU TRY, WELL, YOU JUST WIND UP MAKING MORE ERRORS. SORT OF LIKE A BALL CLUB, YOU KNOW?

BRAD: YEAH, I KNOW. I KNOW. AND IF IT WERE JUST THAT ONE ISOLATED INCIDENT, THERE'D BE NO PROBLEM.

JIM: WHAT D'YOU MEAN? THAT'S THE ONLY TIME I CAN REMEMBER YOU EVER REALLY HAD A PROBLEM WITH MY WORK.

BRAD: JIM—NOW LOOK. I KNOW YOU'RE STILL RELATIVELY NEW WITH THE COMPANY. AND I KNOW THAT WHEN YOU TRANSFERRED INTO OUR SHIFT FROM THE AFTERNOON SHIFT—WELL THAT MADE YOU THE FIRST BLACK GUY ON THE SHIFT. SO I DIDN'T WANNA JUST JUMP ALL OVER YOU. I'VE BEEN TRYING TO GIVE YOU SOME BREATHING ROOM TO GET INTO THE SWING OF THINGS.

JIM: HEY MAN—I KNOW THAT. AND I APPRECIATE IT. WHY DO YOU THINK I GO AROUND ASKING FOR NEW JOBS ALL THE TIME? . . .I'VE BEEN BUSTIN' MY BUTT OUT THERE FOR YOU. I THOUGHT YOU APPRECIATED THAT.

BRAD: JIM, LOOK, I APPRECIATED THE FACT YOU'RE TRYING TO DO JOBS QUICKLY. BUT IT'S EQUALLY IMPORTANT— MAYBE EVEN *MORE* IMPORTANT—TO DO THE JOB CORRECTLY.

Excerpt from "Employment Interviewing"

WALTER: WELL, I THINK I'VE GOT A GOOD FEEL FOR WHAT YOU'VE DONE TO THIS POINT IN YOUR CAREER. YOU'VE OBVIOUSLY BEEN A BUSY PERSON.

JACK: I DO GET A LOT OUT OF MY WORK. I DON'T THINK I'D BE HAPPY IN AN ENVIRONMENT WHERE I WASN'T CHALLENGED: UNDER THE GUN.

WALTER: WE'VE GOT PLENTY OF CHALLENGES HERE, I CAN ASSURE YOU. I'D LIKE TO EXPLORE THIS THEME OF JOB SATISFACTION IN A LITTLE MORE DEPTH. A FEW MOMENTS AGO YOU STATED THAT IN UNDERWRITING SYSTEMS, YOU MUST KNOW AS MUCH OR MORE THAN THE UNDERWRITER HIMSELF. WHAT DID YOU MEAN BY THAT?

JACK: (Very self-assured.) I THOUGHT I DETECTED A RAISED EYEBROW ON THAT COMMENT. LET ME PUT IT THIS WAY: I HAVE TO BE MORE EXACTING THAN AN UNDERWRITER. IF AN UNDERWRITER MAKES A MISTAKE, IT AFFECTS ONLY THAT SINGLE RISK. IF I SCREW UP—EVERYTHING THAT'S IN THE COMPUTER SYSTEM IS WRONG. AND THAT MAKES EVERY POLICY IN THE SYSTEM WRONG. THE MAGNITUDE OF THE ERROR IS GREATER—SO THERE'S A NEED TO BE MORE PRECISE.

WALTER: WHAT GIVES YOU SUCH CONFIDENCE ABOUT YOUR ABILITY IN THE AREA OF UNDERWRITING?

JACK: I KNOW INSURANCE—PLAIN AND SIMPLE. WHEN I STARTED IN PERSONAL LINES

UNDERWRITING WITH THE NATIONAL INDEMNITY, I SEEMED TO CATCH ONTO BASIC PRINCIPLES QUICKLY.

WALTER: WHAT SORT OF TRAINING DID YOU RECEIVE THERE?

JACK: INITIALLY, I WENT THROUGH SEVERAL SELF-STUDY COURSES IN SHORT ORDER. I FOUND I HAD AN APTITUDE FOR IT—SO THE NEXT STEP WAS CPCU COURSES. I'M STILL INTO THAT. IT TAKES AWHILE. . .

WALTER: DON'T I KNOW IT. . .

JACK: BUT I SHOULD BE ABLE TO COMPLETE THE PROGRAM IN ANOTHER YEAR.

WALTER: OK. THAT ACCOUNTS FOR YOUR GROUNDING IN UNDERWRITING? WHAT ABOUT THE SYSTEMS KNOWLEDGE?

JACK: WELL, WITH MY COLLEGE WORK IN COMPUTER SCIENCE AND MATH—IT ALL WORKS TOGETHER IN DEVELOPING AN AUTOMATED COMPUTER SYSTEM FOR A LINE OF BUSINESS. I FEEL AN INTERDISCIPLINARY BACKGROUND IS PERHAPS MY GREATEST STRENGTH IN THIS TYPE WORK.

In nonbroadcast dramatic writing, the writer needs a split personality—half dramatist, half communicator. The excerpt which follows illustrates that balance. The program, designed to introduce a new data system to financial analysts, uses fantasy to dramatize instructional information. A female financial analyst (most of these jobs are held by women) uncovers Aladdin's lamp in her desk at work. A totally contemporary genie appears and will grant three wishes. There's just one catch: since she found the lamp at work, the three wishes must be job-related. We pick up the action after the genie has transported our heroine to a secret cave where he is about to show how a single computer system will answer all three of her wishes.[4]

---

[4]From "Cash & Accounts," written and directed by Jack Pignatello, produced by Thomas H. Salvas for Crum & Forster Corporation. Copyright Crum & Forster Corporation, 1982. Used by permission.

Excerpt from "Cash & Accounts"

GENIE: O.K. I THINK WE'RE HERE—IF I COULD JUST FIND THE. . .YOU KNOW, NOW YOU HAVE *ME* CONFUSED. I ALMOST SAID: "IF I COULD FIND THE LIGHT SWITCH!" I DON'T NEED A LIGHT SWITCH. I'M A GENIE! ALL I HAVE TO DO IS SNAP MY FINGERS.

We hear him snap his fingers. Suddenly the lights go on and we are inside a cave. We see a desk and chair in the center of the room; a computer terminal is on the desk.

She's starting to believe.

KATHY: HOW DID YOU. . .SEE, I'M IMPROVING. I ALMOST SAID. . .

GENIE: "HOW DID YOU DO THAT?"

KATHY: RIGHT. SAY, WHAT IS THIS ON THE DESK?

GENIE: WELL, IT'S A COMPUTER TERMINAL, AND IT'S THE HEART OF A NEW ACCOUNTING SYSTEM CALLED CASH AND ACCOUNTS. EVERYONE IN YOUR DEPARTMENT WILL BE USING IT SOON.

KATHY: CASH AND ACCOUNTS? LIKE THE SECRET PASSWORD?

GENIE: RIGHT—JUST LIKE THE PASSWORD. AND THIS NEW COMPUTER IS ALL I NEED TO GRANT YOU YOUR THREE WISHES.

KATHY: TERRIFIC! INSTEAD OF A GORGEOUS CAR HE GIVES ME A FANCY TYPEWRITER. WHAT AM I GOING TO DO WITH THIS? I DON'T KNOW ANYTHING ABOUT COMPUTERS.

GENIE: THAT'S THE BEAUTY OF THE SYSTEM. YOU REALLY DON'T HAVE TO KNOW ANYTHING ABOUT COMPUTERS.

KATHY: (Very skeptical.) WHAT?

GENIE: REALLY! LOOK, WHY DON'T YOU SIT DOWN. I'LL GIVE YOU A QUICK LESSON.

As she sits down.

KATHY: BUT I DON'T KNOW A COMPUTER TERMINAL FROM A BUS TERMINAL.

GENIE: DID ANYONE EVER TELL YOU THAT YOU'RE A VERY NEGATIVE PERSON?

KATHY: O.K., WISE GUY—SHOW ME!

GENIE: O.K. YOU'RE AN ANALYST, RIGHT? TYPE A-N-A-L-S-T AND HIT THE "ENTER" BUTTON—RIGHT OVER THERE.

KATHY: WHAT?

GENIE: A-N-A-L-S-T AND HIT "ENTER." IT'S THE BUTTON IN THE CORNER. THAT TELLS THE COMPUTER WHAT FUNCTION YOU'RE LOOKING FOR. AND I DIDN'T SPELL "ANALYST" WRONG— THE COMPUTER WILL ONLY ACCEPT

A SIX LETTER CODE, SO WE HAVE
TO ABBREVIATE.

She makes the entry.
The computer
response reads:

"Enter Operator Code   KATHY: O.K. NOW WHAT?
3 Digits"

GENIE: WELL, EVERYONE USING THE
SYSTEM HAS AN OPERATOR CODE.
YOURS WILL BE ONE-TWENTY-
THREE. TYPE "ONE, TWO, THREE"
AND HIT "ENTER."

She does, and the
computer asks:

"Password"   KATHY: NOT ANOTHER PASSWORD.
MY, AREN'T WE SECRETIVE!

GENIE: WELL, THE SYSTEM HAS TO
BE CONFIDENTIAL. YOUR
PRODUCERS ARE *YOURS*. NO ONE
SHOULD HAVE ACCESS TO THEIR
RECORDS EXCEPT YOU. DO YOU
HAVE A NICKNAME?

KATHY: SURE, IT'S ROCKY.

GENIE: O.K. TYPE "ROCKY" AND HIT
"ENTER."

This nuts-and-bolts content typifies many industrial topics. Yet the
presentation maintains audience interest through engaging characterization. Even during the most technical moments, the dialog continues to
reflect the attributes of each character. Kathy and the genie proceed
through the training material in character.

The next sample is illuminating for two reasons. On the surface, it
violates the first principle of writing good dialog. The script (which was
written in the motion picture format) is more one-way speech than a

conversation. Yet, in this case, that is motivated by the fact that the principal character is a high-powered truck salesman. Secondly, in introductory notes, the writer calls for a performance style that is bigger than life:

> Delivery is very fast for the first instructor, and speech has been scripted in a disjointed style—taking off from the transcripts. This is a long program (24 minutes) but not a slow one.

Imagine the effect of the following material delivered in a rapid-fire pace.[5]

Excerpt from "Good Ideas on Hot Prospecting"

4.   ECU OF STACK OF PROSPECTING MATERIAL.

FIRST INSTRUCTOR:

Forget all this. . .

SWEEPS STACKS UNCEREMON-
IOUSLY OFF THE TABLE.

. . .let's get down to the nitty-gritty on
how to use the phone to make a living.

PULLS A PHONE OUT FROM BE-
NEATH THE TABLE AND PLUNKS
IT DOWN CAMERA CENTER.

What's the one-to-one? What do I say
on the phone to a guy. . . who doesn't
know me, who may hate me, who is busy,
who has to go to the bathroom; you
know, there are a million reasons why this
guy doesn't want to talk to me.

CUT TO. . .

---

[5]From "Good Ideas on Hot Prospecting," written by Randall Garrison, directed by Lawrence Perry, produced by Regan Productions, Inc. for GMC Truck and Coach Operations, Truck and Bus Group, General Motors Corporation. Used by permission.

5.   SECOND INSTRUCTOR LEANING FORWARD.

> **SECOND INSTRUCTOR:**
> We're supposed to train the salesman
> in what to say. . .

CUT TO. . .

6.   FIRST INSTRUCTOR LEANING BACK.

> **FIRST INSTRUCTOR**:
> Well, I think it's more important. . .yeah,
> probably (LEANS FORWARD) what we
> *should* be doing is *train the salesman in
> what to think up*, to write down on his little
> piece of paper; find these three things you
> can tell people; use this three-step procedure
> to get a sale, a name or an appointment.
> (PICKS UP THE PHONE) Now if I'm
> going to pick up a phone and I'm going to
> call a person I don't know. . .*why* am I
> going to call you? What am I going to say to
> you? (TOYS WITH THE PHONE) You
> know I'm gonna offer you dance lessons. . .or
> I'm going to offer you a free meal to come
> look at our property in the north or. . .I'm
> gonna have something, in theory, that I'm
> going to have to say. (PUTS THE PHONE
> BACK DOWN, LEANS TOWARD
> SECOND INSTRUCTOR) Well, what does
> a truck salesman say? A truck salesman has
> to say something like we just doubled the
> size of our service department and I'd like
> you to come down and take a look at it, you
> know at our. . .

CUT TO. . .

7.   SECOND INSTRUCTOR; GESTURES THE "HOOK."

> **SECOND INSTRUCTOR**
> There has to be a hook is what you're saying.

CUT TO. . .

8.   FIRST INSTRUCTOR; REPEATING GESTURE.

> **FIRST INSTRUCTOR**:
> . . .there has to be a hook. We've gotten a shipment of four dump trucks; we don't need dump trucks and we're trying to get rid of the dump trucks; can you use a dump truck, you know, that kind of thing. . .

CUT TO. . .

9.   SECOND INSTRUCTOR.

> **SECOND INSTRUCTOR**:
> "I got a special on dump trucks."

CUT TO. . .

10.   FIRST INSTRUCTOR.

> **FIRST INSTRUCTOR**:
>
> I got a used, you know, Cummins, et cetera; which I think would be really great in the construction business and I'm tryin' to find a home for it; can you use this truck? Do you know somebody who could use this truck? Can you give me the name of somebody? O.K., then you say "I can't use it" and then to get me off your back, you say, "Talk to Barney Smaltz" so then I call Barney Smaltz. . .

DRAWS ON CHALKBOARD:

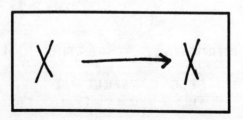

. . .and I say *you* gave me Barney's name
and said he might be interested in this truck;
now I've got an intro. I've gotten a name; if I
can't get a sale, I've gotten a name.

DRAWS ON CHALKBOARD:

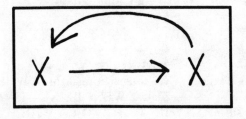

Then I call *you* back and I say, "Talked to
Barney and he's really not interested in it,
but I want to thank you for giving me that
name and I'd like to tell you later when we
get another one of these things in or I'd like
to come over and look at your operation
some time, stop in on my way home," or
whatever. . .

DRAWS ON CHALKBOARD:

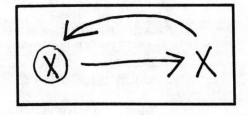

. . .I try to build a contact. . .

In this high-density information piece, every single word relates directly
to the subject at hand. Yet the dialog remains in character at all times and
establishes credibility.

A final example illustrates a functional use of dialog and human
behavior to convey less didactic content. The two scenes that follow are
from a program used in training employment interviewers to objectively

evaluate handicapped job applicants. These scenes show a blind job
applicant, Craig Cunningham, with his wife on a Sunday afternoon. The
next morning, Craig is scheduled for a follow-up interview with a major
corporation. Both the dialog and the action were selected to contradict
common stereotypes of what blind people can do.[6]

Excerpt from "Why Not Craig Cunningham?"

FADE UP ON:

ESTABLISHING SHOT showing Craig with his wife Maureen. They are sitting down to a leisurely Sunday brunch. They talk animatedly as we listen to Maureen's voice-over commentary.	MAUREEN: (Voice-over in a reflective, yet conversational tone.) WHEN CRAIG FIRST WENT BLIND—I WAS REALLY UP-TIGHT FOR A WHILE. I GUESS IT WAS ANXIETY MORE THAN ANYTHING. I KNEW IT WAS CHANGING OUR LIVES. . .MAYBE EVEN OUR MARRIAGE. IT'D HAPPENED. BANG! THERE WAS NO CHANGING IT. ALL OF A SUDDEN, I FELT LIKE OUR LIVES HAD GONE OUT OF CONTROL—WHERE WOULD IT EVENTUALLY TAKE US? MOST OF ALL, I WORRIED ABOUT HOW IT WOULD CHANGE HIM AS A PERSON. IT WASN'T UNTIL *I* ACCEPTED THE FACT THAT THIS IS THE SAME CRAIG CUNNINGHAM I MARRIED, ONLY NOW HE HAPPENS TO BE BLIND, THAT THE ANXIETY FINALLY WENT AWAY.
	SURE, IT CHANGED OUR LIVES—IN LOTS OF WAYS. CERTAINLY FOR NOW, WE'RE MORE FINANCIALLY DEPENDENT ON MY JOB TRYING TO GET SEVENTH GRADERS TO WRITE

---

[6]From "Why Not Craig Cunningham?" written by William Van Nostran, directed by Barry Byrne, produced by William J. Benham for AT&T Corporate Television. Used by permission.

A GRAMMATICALLY CORRECT
SENTENCE. BECAUSE OF THAT—
WE'VE PUT OFF HAVING KIDS. IN
FACT, WE'VE SORT OF TABLED
THAT INDEFINITELY.

BUT EVEN THOUGH SOME BIG
THINGS LIKE THAT CHANGED, AND
WE BOTH HAD A LOT TO LEARN
ABOUT COPING WITH HIS
DISABILITY—I CAN HONESTLY SAY
THAT WE'VE GOTTEN BACK INTO
PRETTY MUCH OF A NORMAL
ROUTINE. LITTLE THINGS HAVEN'T
CHANGED THAT MUCH. CRAIG
STILL LOVES TO HELP MAKE A BIG
SUNDAY MORNING BRUNCH. . .

DISSOLVE TO:

MS—as Maureen and
Craig do dishes and
and talk quietly.

AND WE STILL DO DISHES
TOGETHER AFTERWARDS SINCE MY
SAVINGS FUND FOR A DISHWASHER
ALWAYS TURNS INTO NEXT WEEK'S
LUNCH MONEY. . .

MAUREEN: ABOUT TIME WE GOT
SOME DECENT WEATHER ON A
SUNDAY.

CRAIG: I'VE BEEN MEANING TO
WASH AND WAX THE CAR—LOOKS
LIKE I'VE GOT NO EXCUSE TODAY.

MAUREEN: THAT'S ONE
HOUSEHOLD CHORE YOU'VE
LEARNED TO DO THAT TRULY
AMAZES ME.

CRAIG: HEY, IT'S JUST CRAIG
CUNNINGHAM AND HIS AMAZING
KINETIC MEMORY.

MAUREEN: HOW COME CRAIG
CUNNINGHAM AND HIS "AMAZING
KINETIC MEMORY" NEVER TEAM UP

TO TAKE THE GARBAGE OUT?
ANSWER ME THAT!

CRAIG: C'MON, HONEY—WHAT
GOOD IS IT BEING HANDICAPPED IF
YOU DON'T LEARN TO USE IT TO
YOUR ADVANTAGE? BE GLAD I
DERIVE SO MUCH PLEASURE FROM
DRYING DISHES.

MAUREEN: I'VE GOT TO ADMIT, FOR
THE LONGEST TIME I THOUGHT I
WAS DOOMED TO A LIFETIME OF
SOLITARY DISHWASHING. YOU
HAVE MADE PROGRESS.

CRAIG: JUST THAT ONE SLUMP
WHEN I BROKE ABOUT FOUR
GLASSES IN THE SPACE OF TWO
DAYS "HELPING" WITH THE DISHES.

MAUREEN: YEAH, BUT CRAIG—YOU
BROKE GLASSES WHEN YOU COULD
SEE. MY MOTHER USED TO LOCK
THE GOOD ONES UP WHEN YOU
CAME OVER.

CRAIG: ONCE A KLUTZ, ALWAYS A
KLUTZ.

MAUREEN: (Changing the subject after a
lull.) YOU WANT TO GO OUT
ANYWHERE THIS AFTERNOON?

CRAIG: NOT UNLESS YOU DO. I
MIGHT RUN LATER.

MAUREEN: I JUST THOUGHT MAYBE
YOU'D WANT TO STAY BUSY SO THE
DAY GOES BY FASTER.

CRAIG: IT'LL GO FAST ENOUGH IF I
DO THE CAR. . .BESIDES, THERE'S A
GAME ON THIS AFTERNOON.

MAUREEN: SOONER OR LATER I GUESS I'VE GOTTA GRADE PAPERS. . .BE GLAD WHEN SUMMER VACATION GETS HERE THIS YEAR. . .

CRAIG: JUST KEEP THE DISHES COMING, WOULD YA? THE BLIND WORKER'S GETTING BORED WITH THIS.

MAUREEN: (Voice-over) CERTAINLY I'LL NEVER REALLY KNOW ALL THAT CRAIG EXPERIENCED LEARNING TO COPE WITH BEING BLIND. FOR MYSELF—WELL, I HAD TO LEARN NOT TO BE OVERPROTECTIVE. IN THE BEGINNING, IT WAS DIFFICULT. I KNOW NOW THAT IF HE NEEDS HELP—HE'LL ASK. OTHERWISE, I LET HIM FEND FOR HIMSELF. IT'S INTERESTING. . .SOMETIMES WHEN I THINK ABOUT OUR DAILY CONVERSATIONS, IT'S NOT LIKE YOU COULD TELL HE'S BLIND OR I'M SIGHTED. . .

FADE UP ON Craig in living room—he's "watching" a ball-game on TV.

MAUREEN: (Her head appearing from a doorway down the hall.) HEY, HONEY, HAVE YOU SEEN WHERE I PUT THOSE PAPERS I HAVE TO GRADE? I'M GETTING AS DISORGANIZED AS YOU.

CRAIG: WERE THEY IN A BUNCH OF FILE FOLDERS?

MAUREEN: UH-HUH. . .

CRAIG: TRY THE SPARE ROOM. . .

MAUREEN: I'M *IN* THE SPARE ROOM. . .

CRAIG: CHECK UNDER MY DIGICASSETTE BY THE TYPING STAND.

MAUREEN: WHAT INNING IS IT?

CRAIG: TOP OF THE FIFTH, REDS JUST TIED IT UP. . .YOU FIND YOUR PAPERS?

MAUREEN: (Coming into the room with papers.) YES, I FOUND *MY* PAPERS, BURIED UNDER *YOUR* JUNK.

CRAIG: (Rises, goes into kitchen.) JUNK TO YOU, MAYBE. I'M GONNA GET A BEER—WANT ANYTHING?

MAUREEN: NO THANKS—STILL FULL FROM BRUNCH. WHAT SUIT ARE YOU WEARING TOMORROW?

CRAIG: (From the kitchen.) I GUESS THE BLUE ONE. THEY SAY IT'S GONNA WARM UP TOMORROW. (Sticks his head back in the room.) HOW ABOUT POPCORN? WANT ME TO MAKE SOME POPCORN?

MAUREEN: CRAIG, I'M ON A DIET AGAIN.

CRAIG: YEAH, I NOTICED AT BRUNCH.

MAUREEN: YOU CAN EAT ANYTHING YOU WANT EARLY IN THE DAY—IT'S LATER IN THE DAY THAT YOU'VE GOT TO COUNT CALORIES. . .

CRAIG: THAT'S YOUR MOTHER TALKING. . .

MAUREEN: LISTEN. . .REMIND ME TO STICK A BLUE SHIRT IN THE WASH FOR YOUR BIG INTERVIEW TOMORROW.

CRAIG: (Moves behind her and puts his arms around her.) HEY HONEY. . .

MAUREEN: (Feigns ignoring him and concentrates on papers.) YEAH. . .

CRAIG: DON'T FORGET TO STICK A BLUE SHIRT IN THE WASH FOR ME. . .

MAUREEN: (Looking up to him and laughing.) NOT NOW. . .LATER. REMIND ME LATER.

NARRATIVE COMBINATIONS

Once the writer gains a facility for developing characters and dramatic situations, the same techniques can be folded into more traditional narrative forms. Conventional narration can be used to comment on the dramatic action and offer additional information. Certain types of content may suggest parodies or fables as a means of conveying information on screen. Quiz show parodies, for example, have often been used to meet sales training objectives. Character-voice narrations can put an editorial slant on a subject which may not be possible with the more traditional spokesperson. In a presentation on the use of a microfiche system, for example, the subject was explained by a "mild-mannered computer programmer" transformed into Microman—"visitor from a microscopic planet." Cartoon style artwork depicted this fictional character, a takeoff on the super hero.

In a more traditional vein, historical figures, the founders of a major insurance holding company, were brought to life in a new employee orientation.[1]

---

[7]From "Crum and Forster Orientation," written and produced by William Van Nostran, directed by James G. Libby. Copyright Crum & Forster Corporation, 1982. Used by permission.

Excerpt from "Crum and Forster Orientation"

	NARRATOR: THE FIRE OF 1835, AS WELL AS SIMILAR FIRES IN NEW YORK, CHICAGO AND SAN FRANCISCO, BROUGHT ABOUT REFORMS AND MORE SOPHISTICATED UNDERWRITING PRACTICES.
	FOR INSTANCE:
Map of the times with dots to illustrate risks in many geographic areas	IF INSURANCE IS A MEANS OF SPREADING RISK, THEN INDIVIDUAL COMPANIES SHOULD NOT ACCEPT ALL THEIR FIRE POLICIES FROM A SINGLE AREA OF ONE CITY. COMPANIES WERE BETTER ABLE TO SUSTAIN LOSSES BY BALANCING THEIR BOOK OF BUSINESS TO INCLUDE RISKS FROM MANY CITIES AND GEOGRAPHIC AREAS.
Shot of Crum and Forster.	WE BEGAN THE C&F STORY WITH A LOOK AT THE NORTH RIVER COMPANY BECAUSE THAT'S WHERE THE ASSOCIATION BETWEEN MR. CRUM AND MR. FORSTER STARTED. THEY WERE BOTH NORTH RIVER EMPLOYEES. JOHN FORSTER WAS ENERGETIC AND ENTHUSIASTIC— SOMETHING OF AN IDEA MAN. HE EXPLAINS THE IDEA BEHIND THE VENTURE WHICH LAUNCHED CRUM & FORSTER IN 1896:
ECU on Forster's portrait.	VOICE OF JOHN FORSTER: THE ORIGINAL IDEA WAS SIMPLE ENOUGH—FREDERICK CRUM, JAMES ACKERMAN AND I WOULD
SUPER:	FORM A PARTNERSHIP TO OPEN AN
John Forster	INSURANCE AGENCY AND REPRE-

SENT THE ALLEMANNIA FIRE
INSURANCE COMPANY IN THE NEW
YORK CITY AREA. AFTER ALL, WE
WERE KNOWLEDGEABLE OF THE
NEW YORK CITY MARKET FOR FIRE
INSURANCE IN THOSE TIMES—AND
WE KNEW THE HAZARDS
INVOLVED. SO WE WERE IN A
POSITION TO PLACE GOOD RISKS
WITH THE ALLEMANNIA. . .

ECU on Crum's
portrait.

SUPER:

Frederick Crum

VOICE OF FREDERICK CRUM: WE
STARTED THE BUSINESS WITH JUST
$501, IN SPACE RENTED FROM OUR
FORMER EMPLOYER—THE NORTH
RIVER. BUT WITHIN TEN YEARS WE
WERE ACTING AS AGENTS FOR A
HOST OF COMPANIES, INCLUDING
THE UNITED STATES FIRE
INSURANCE COMPANY—WHICH
HAD A FINE AGENCY OPERATION. . .

Thinking Like a Playwright

The writer who can successfully create characters and bring them to life will find innumerable applications for such techniques in corporate, medical and educational subjects. As with any technique, their use should be justified based on an assessment of audience, objectives and content. Research for such assignments will often center on behavior and speech patterns in addition to specific content. In preparing for the program on handicapped employees, for instance, the writer held several interviews with disabled people to learn about their capabilities, attitudes and experiences interacting with ablebodied people.

Finally, when constructing the nonbroadcast drama, the writer needs to think like a playwright. This chapter began with a scenario of what *preceded* an on-camera scene to illustrate that, when it comes to drama, the writer must know the history of the characters in order to bring them to life. By imitating human action, the writer gains a powerful tool for creating audience involvement.

11

Writing For Interactive Video

Interactive video—programming that goes beyond passive viewing by building in activities that the viewer must perform—is the new "darling" of the nonbroadcast field. These days, interactive hardware and software are the focal point of every industry trade show. Seminars and workshops to teach interactive program design are everywhere you turn. It's like a kid discovering a new toy.

Ironically, the concept of interactive video has been kicking around in a variety of forms for years. Still more irony: one of the earliest examples of an interactive video application was a broadcast program back in television's golden age, the 1950s. *Winky-Dink and You*, a children's show, encouraged young viewers to participate by drawing Winky's weekly form on a sheet of acetate placed over the TV screen.

Other broadcast examples followed. Network television has used interactive techniques for involving viewers in subjects such as driver safety or identifying their own heart attack risk. And, in cable TV, Warner Amex's experiments with Qube, a two-way cable system, introduced interaction on a community level. Qube offers not only 30 channels of programming, but five response buttons for communicating viewer reactions. Through the cable connection, viewer responses flow into a computer in the studio for an instantaneous audience poll. In addition to responding on issues of local importance, viewers were invited to select covers for upcoming issues of *Us* magazine or call plays for a local football team scrimmage.

HISTORICAL PERSPECTIVE

However, what is genuinely new in nonbroadcast interactive video and what has generated the intense marketplace interest is the concurrent growth of three synergistic technologies: programmed instruction, the video disc and minicomputers. To place these developments in perspective, let's trace the evolution of nonbroadcast training programming. The advent of the video cassette in 1972 led to rapid growth of private nonbroadcast video networks, which trainers used in one of three ways. The first and most basic application was to use video as a playback device for the traditional classroom film. Second, video tape's instant record-playback capability gave trainers a useful tool for behavioral training. Sales training or public speaking courses, for instance, used video tape to record a student's performance for instantaneous playback, observation and analysis by teacher and student alike.

The third early application used the private networks to distribute self-study training materials. Sending training programs where they were needed in the field gave greater leverage to many understaffed training departments. Savings in travel and greater flexibility in responding to training needs in a timely fashion resulted. Quite often, however, this meant no more than video taping existing classroom lectures, an approach that proved less than successful. First, the original presentation was structured, formatted and paced for live presentation in the classroom instead of being structured for video's time-space continuum. Second, the viewer remained passive, uninvolved; unable to ask questions, apply concepts or test comprehension. In short, trainers required better mechanisms to insure instructional objectives were met. Program design that permitted participation provided the answer.

Early Modes of Interaction

The earliest modes of nonbroadcast interactive programming borrowed the principles of Programmed Instructional (PI) materials. This highly structured form of self-study, which grew out of World War II training needs, breaks content into small, bite-sized learning points that are mastered one at a time in sequential order. Programmed Instructional learning is self-pacing as the learner works individually with the materials, which may be as simple as a single workbook. The PI format involves frequent testing (multiple-choice, true/false, fill-ins, etc.) to ensure the learner masters each point before being allowed to move on to new material. Reinforcement is achieved through repetition.

Early PI courses often used audio-visual media to present concepts and clarify content. So with the growth of the video cassette as a corporate training tool, adapting principles of programmed instruction to video cassette programming was a natural evolution. One pioneering effort to explain the mechanics of interactive program design is found in Barwick and Kranz's *The Compleat Videocassette User's Guide*,[1] which devoted an entire chapter to interactive program design principles. Figure 11.1 illustrates the structure of an interactive program of that day, which consisted of two distinct parts, online and offline.

Figure 11.1: Structure of Early Interactive Programs

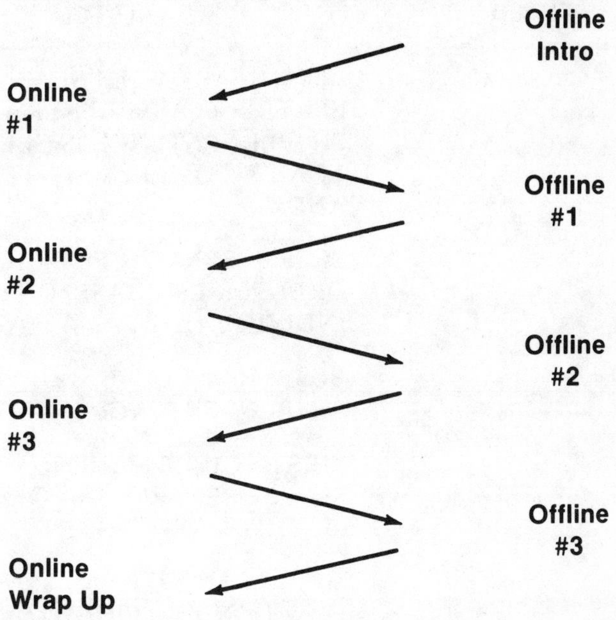

Based on "A Diagram of a Typical Videorecord Lesson Unit," in *The Compleat Videocassette User's Guide*, p.63.

The online segment, in which most new information was first presented to the learner, equates to video content. Offline activities took place away from the TV screen. As a general rule, offline activities gave the learner

[1]John Barwick and Stewart Kranz, *The Compleat Videocassette User's Guide: Principles and Practice of Programming* (White Plains, NY: Knowledge Industry Publications, Inc., 1973).

an opportunity to put new knowledge to use in workbook exercises, readings, simulations, physical tasks or role playing as appropriate to the specific learning process at hand. To illustrate, look at the following example of an interactive program on how to write business correspondence. First, the video script presents the online activity.[2]

Excerpt from "Letter Writing Workshop"

VIDEO	AUDIO
MS—On Narrator.	LET'S START WITH SIMPLICITY IN A SENTENCE. AS A GENERAL RULE, A SIMPLE SENTENCE IS CLEARER THAN A COMPLEX SENTENCE, AND. . .
	SIMPLE SENTENCES PLACE GREATER EMPHASIS ON EACH INDIVIDUAL IDEA.
	BUT WHAT DO WE MEAN BY A SIMPLE SENTENCE?
	FIRST—OUR DEFINITION OF A SIMPLE SENTENCE IS THAT IT CONTAINS ONLY ONE INDEPENDENT CLAUSE.
	NOW DON'T BE FRIGHTENED BY THIS LINGUISTIC JARGON.
	TO PUT IT ANOTHER WAY, A SIMPLE SENTENCE CONTAINS ONLY ONE THOUGHT.
	PERHAPS THIS CAN BE ILLUSTRATED BEST BY EXAMINING A POORLY CONSTRUCTED AND UNNECESSARILY COMPLEX SENTENCE.

---

[2]From "Letter Writing Workshop," written by William Van Nostran and Donna Galer, directed by Dick DeMaio for Crum & Forster Corporation. Copyright Crum & Forster Corporation 1978, 1982. Used by permission.

VIDEO	AUDIO
	PAGE 11 OF YOUR WORKBOOK CONTAINS A SHORT ACTIVITY DESIGNED TO HELP YOU MASTER THE CONCEPT OF SIMPLE SENTENCES.
CU—On slide of building blocks.	THE EXCERISE INVOLVES THIS SENTENCE. YOUR TASK IS TO DETERMINE HOW MANY DISTINCT THOUGHTS ARE CONTAINED IN THE SENTENCE.
CRAWL SUPER [Lines of text move from bottom to top of screen]: "I have been advised that this firm carries a fine Dun & Bradstreet rating of CB2 and we would be happy to review additional financial information from this firm to aid in our decision-making process, for example, would you submit along with any additional comments the last three financial reports for this firm."	YOUR WORKBOOK TELLS YOU HOW TO DIVIDE THE SENTENCE INTO SEPARATE THOUGHTS. WHEN YOU'VE COMPLETED THIS ACTIVITY, CONTINUE WITH THE VIDEO CONTENT. NOW STOP THE TAPE.

The learner then turns to this offline activity in the workbook.:

Tape Exercise IV: Simple Sentences

Read the following sentence and put a double slash mark after each distinct thought.

For example: He finished the renewals// there were ten cancellations.

Now do the following exercise:

I have been advised that this firm carries a fine Dun & Bradstreet rating of CB2 and we would be happy to review additional financial information from this firm to aid in our decision-making process, for example, would you submit along with any additional comments the last three financial reports for this firm.

START TAPE

Notice that with the offline activity, we've come full circle, returning to writing for print as well as for a viewing experience. Of course the online and offline materials must function as a unified, integrated whole, so that basic concepts explained in the online program are reinforced through offline activities.

A MARRIAGE OF TECHNOLOGIES

Although the online/offline format has proven useful for many applications, it seems primitive in light of current technology. The newest forms of interactive programming and the potential they hold for instructional designers result from the synergy among the minicomputer, the video disc and the concept of programed instruction.

The use of the computer as a teaching machine or electronic tutor goes back to the 1960s. In computer-assisted instruction (CAI), instructional content is stored within a computer. Using a cathode-ray tube (CRT) TV terminal and a typewriter-like keyboard or pad, this content can be presented interactively, including tests or quizzes to insure mastery of subject matter. This interaction differs dramatically from early interactive video programs because it remains online. Instead of turning to a workbook, the learner responds directly to questions by typing on the keyboard. Both questions and answers are displayed on the CRT.

Additionally, the computer program can be written so the learner's responses or choices trigger the computer's next move. In this way each learner devises a unique path through the content. Instruction is nonlinear and individualized, allowing a student to repeat material that proves difficult or skip information already mastered. Furthermore, student responses can be collected and stored in the computer for analysis and evaluation.

However, there are drawbacks. Visuals are limited to text, numbers or simple schematics and line drawings. Furthermore, audio is not part of this learning experience. The introduction of video discs changed things dramatically. The capabilities of video discs were described in Chapter 2. But to reiterate their significance for programed instruction, optical video disc features and their benefits to the instructional designer are summarized in Figure 11.2. The most revolutionary feature is the direct computer interface: a sophisticated computer can talk to a video disc player—and control its functions. Now, the audio-visual potential of television can be combined with the interactive branching potential and instructional software of CAI. Figure 11.3 shows an interactive video learning station.

Figure 11.2: Optical Video Disc Features that Aid Instructional Design

Feature	Benefit
54,000 separate frame locations	The video disc is an information storage/retrieval system. It permits high-density storage and retrieval of information in various formats: text; video tape; film; artwork; slides or other still images.
Random access	Average access time from frame to frame is 2.5 seconds. This greatly facilitates nonlinear sequencing.
Scan (forward or reverse)	Permits the user to screen program material rapidly to find a specific segment.
Still frame and slow motion controls	Allows the viewer to analyze motion in detail. Could also facilitate note taking or detailed study of a single frame or sequence of frames.
Direct computer interface	A special connector permits access to the disc player's internal microcomputer from an external computer.

The New Interaction

In the early 1980s, this marriage of video disc and computer technology spurred an explosion of interest in more sophisticated interactive video. In addition to traditional instructional applications such as programmed learning, the technology opens the door to other applications that require a random access computer-driven program. A video disc catalog with product demos and ordering information, for example, is already in use right down the street at your General Motors dealership. Instructions for assembling electronics kits may some day be available on interactive video discs. Interactive cookbooks will present Julia Child recipes one step at a time.

Up to this point, we've discussed creating traditional linear scripts. Even the early interactive programs were essentially linear: Online Viewing 1 led the learner to Offline Activity 1, which led to Online Viewing 2 and so on, to

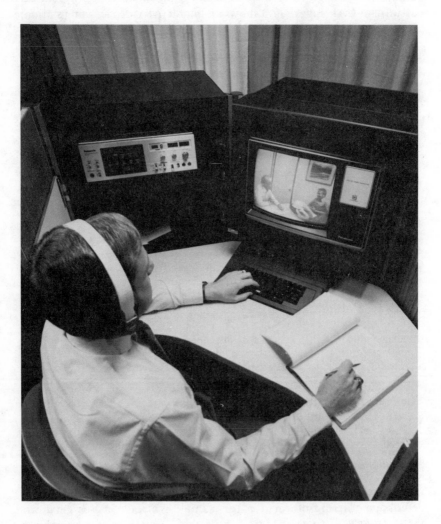

Figure 11.3 At a modern interactive study carrel, the learner uses video disc and microcomputer technology—as well as an old-fashioned workbook. Courtesy Synsor Corporation.

the end of the program. The combined capabilities of video disc and microprocessor, however, offer both the program designer and the individual user great flexibility to move through a program in a random, nonlinear sequence. Perhaps the simplest illustration of the concept of nonlinear programming is the traditional computer menu for informational retrieval. Nothing more than an electronic index, the computer menu allows a user to locate specific information and display it on the CRT screen.

Suppose, for instance, a computer/video disc system stored maps of major cities, and we need to find the location of a Wall Street address. We will sequence through a series of menus, starting with major cities.

Major Cities	Computer Index
Atlanta	01
Boston	02
Buffalo	03
Cleveland	04
Dallas	05
Houston	06
Los Angeles	07
New York	08

By typing "08" on the keyboard, we are presented with another menu, offering still more branching possibilities.

New York City (08)

Borough	Computer Index
Brooklyn	8-1
Bronx	8-2
Manhattan	8-3
Queens	8-4
Staten Island	8-5

Surrounding Areas

Long Island	8-6
Connecticut	8-7
New Jersey	8-8

Since we know the Wall Street financial district is in lower Manhattan, we would enter "8-3" and find yet another menu.

Borough of Manhattan (NYC) 8-3

District	Computer Index
Uptown	
East Side	8-31A
West Side	8-31B
Midtown	
East Side	8-32A
West Side	8-32B
Special Theater District	8-32C
Lower Manhattan	
Greenwich Village	8-33A
City Hall Area	8-33B
Wall Street/Battery	8-33C

By entering "8-33C," we would see, for the first time, a map instead of another computer menu. Obviously, with this information retrieval system, there's no single linear path through the information. The user's need at the time dictates the progression. Much information may be skipped completely. In General Motors showrooms, for example, the salesman or the consumer can use the video disc catalog to find information only for the specific make, model or feature (such as gas mileage or options) the consumer is interested in.

Branching: an Interactive Training Technique

The same principle is put to use in interactive training programs using the video disc and minicomputer. However, rather than discretionary branching, where the user determines which information to access, the computer is programmed to route the learner through the appropriate material based upon the learner's response to questions, quizzes or other types of interaction. The computer diagnoses the individual learner's needs, then directs the learner to appropriate segments on the video disc. The computer's function as facilitator is illustrated by a common technique in interactive training program design, the pre-test, which covers all program content in a comprehensive quiz. Individual student answers tell the computer what material is already understood and, more importantly, which material needs detailed explanation.

Assume, for sake of illustration, that you take a pre-test consisting of ten multiple-choice questions. Of those ten, you answer three incorrectly. The computer begins instruction with a module relating to the first question missed. That content would then be followed by a more detailed quiz on the subject. Suppose you still answer one question incorrectly. In that event, the same instructional unit might be replayed in its entirety. Or, in a more sophisticated sequence, the computer might branch you into another module that replays only material pertaining to the missed question. In an even more sophisticated program, the computer might route the learner to an in-depth treatment of the material to provide better comprehension of subject matter.

The computer can be programmed to continue to repeat or to branch to remedial sections until the learner demonstrates mastery of the specific subject matter. Only then will the computer take the learner to new subject matter. Finally, a summary post-test might follow, sending the learner back to any material not retained. This is a distinct plus compared to conventional formats where the learner controls pace and sequencing. In programmed instructional workbooks, for instance, the learner can skip over material that should be reviewed in detail or waste time on material that is already understood. By contrast, the computer gives the trainer or instructor more control of the individualized learning process.

IMPLICATIONS FOR THE WRITER

Clearly, writing the script for an interactive training program using video disc, computer and software package requires conceptual and organizational skills quite distinct from those required for straightforward linear presentations. Rather than writing a script, the writer performs the role of program designer—assessing the training task, setting instructional objectives and formatting the array of interactions and reinforcements necessary to build skills and test comprehension. The writer now finds himself in collaboration not only with a producer and director, but also with a computer programmer.

To carry out the task successfully, the author must conduct traditional research to discover what needs to be communicated, to whom, for what purpose. In addition, although the writer may not actually program computer software or translate film/video frames into video disc index numbers, he or she will certainly need to understand how these processes interrelate and what capabilities or limitations are inherent in the hardware/software package in use.

ADAPTING TO NEW DEMANDS

This chapter is not intended to explore the nuts and bolts of writing and designing interactive video disc programs but to shed light on interactive video applications and the demands of writing a nonlinear script. (If you need to know more, I recommend the *Handbook of Interactive Video* by Steve and Beth Floyd.[3]) However, a few common sense principles are offered as general advice.

Don't Overlook Other Forms of Interaction

As with any new technology, there is a temptation to go overboard and pull out all the stops. In truth, not all subjects require a video disc/computer package. In general, this teaching tool is best suited to objective, factual content where there are clear-cut right or wrong answers; yes and no, or go/no-go decisions. It is less appropriate for subjective, behavioral content involving value judgments or interpretations with shades of gray.

There is nothing wrong with forms of interactive video which are not computer assisted. The online/offline model is still useful—especially in those cases where a video presentation is integrated into live instruction. For other subjects, the use of offline activities may be best facilitated without the use of a computer. A programmed learning cookbook, for instance, probably needs only interactions that take place in the kitchen using the real thing. Other subjects, such as teaching report or letter writing, may still be best suited to offline workbook activities involving writing assignments. In these instances, computer interaction might be an intrusion.

Learn the Capabilities of the System

As mentioned previously, if a video disc/computer hardware package is deemed best suited to the content, learn the capabilities of the system inside and out. Find out exactly what types of interaction are possible and how sophisticated the opportunities for branching are. Learn how content must be sequenced and how the computer and video display capabilities interrelate. Because each hardware/software package is different, you can't make assumptions about what is or is not possible. As program designer, it's your business to know the package. Also, remember that the more you plan interactively, the more costly the project is likely to become—not just in software programming but in the possible need for video footage to match a variety of scenarios accompanying branching possibilities.

---

[3]Steve Floyd and Beth Floyd, eds., *Handbook of Interactive Video* (White Plains, NY: Knowledge Industry Publications, Inc., 1982).

Don't Overdesign

Subject matter should dictate the complexity of branching, the types of interaction and the frequency of interaction. Clearly, an interactive program used for pilot training on small aircraft will need to be more complex than a program which offers driver safety tips. The latter may be quite simple and straightforward in design. You needn't use the total capabilities of an interactive system in every project.

Design Appropriate Interactions

Multiple-choice questions or true-false quizzes may be quite appropriate for some subjects, totally inappropriate for others. The combined capabilities of the video disc and most computer programs offer a myriad of potential types of interaction or reinforcement. Case study situations can be simulated using action footage or graphics. Questions can be devised to encourage the learner to analyze what is happening on the screen and select "what happens next" based on a menu of alternative choices. Another form of interaction could involve labeling component parts on an engineering schematic. The type of interaction selected should be based on the nature of the subject matter, objectives and the audience profile.

Think and Organize in Nonlinear Fashion

As a program designer, you'll need to develop techniques for structuring material in discrete, finite units. The interrelationships between these units, especially when branching or sophisticated testing is involved, become crucial. As always, of course, good program design will begin with a comprehensive set of instructional objectives, an audience profile and a content outline. Analyze content and objectives to determine how many objectives can be covered in specific learning modules or sequences. Then brainstorm the types of interaction that can be devised to reinforce concepts; offer skill-building applications or test for comprehension before moving on to new material.

Early in the conceptual process, you'll need to develop a system for identifying points of interaction and branching possibilities. Still more critical is a system for diagramming the multiple paths of your program design as individual viewers thread their way through content based on their own choices. Given the random access capabilities of today's video discs and minicomputers and the complexity of many nonbroadcast topics, organizing your interactive "tree" and identifying where all "branches" take the viewer can be a Herculean task. But this step is an essential prerequisite for actual scripting.

To illustrate step-by-step progressions and be able to communicate program branches to collaborators, many instructional designers use a flowcharts, sets of symbols connecting lines to depict the interactive organization. Excerpts from a sample flowchart for one writer's interactive video disc program are shown in Figure 11.4. The flowchart was created for *Think It Through*, a series of programs intended to help build the problem-solving and decision-making skills of hearing-impaired children. This program is in the form of a mystery, in which food coloring disappears from a grocery store. (For more on the project, see the interview with writer and instructional designer Casey Stone in Chapter 12.)

The complexity of the flowchart, even for this relatively simple content, illustrates why some form of flowcharting is essential for even the most rudimentary interactive branching. The superstructure for the script involves three stages—definition of the problem, possible solutions and evaluating solutions. The author uses a TV screen shape as a symbol for video program content and rectangles to indicate information appearing on the screen as text and decision blocks. Some branches become dead ends that automatically take the viewer back to an earlier point in the decision-making tree.

Another interesting aspect of this flowchart is that there is more than a single right answer. The child who reasons correctly through either branch is rewarded for "correctly" solving the mystery, even though the two branches arrive at different answers.

If you become involved in designing an interactive program, you will need to devise a similar format for charting individual branches and paths. As a preparatory step to flowcharting, consider using file cards, similar to those used in structuring an unscripted program, as a way of plotting out branching possibilities. Label each file card as either a discrete video program element or bit of video text information. As you organize these file cards, laying them out on a table or a bulletin board, you'll be creating your own flowchart. With file cards, you can easily revise certain branches or try out various branching patterns. The important point is that until the entire interactive structure is systematically charted, it's impossible to begin writing the video scripts.

Develop Functional Formats

You'll also want to develop treatment and script formats that are functional in terms of the interactions you plan. One interactive producer, Peter Crown, suggests this technique:

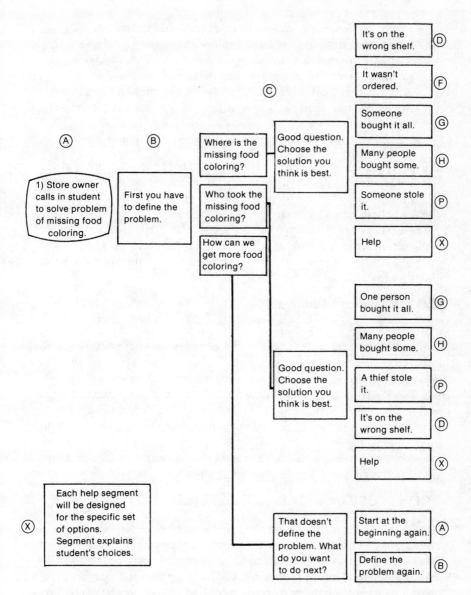

Figure 11.4 The branching of the interactive program for the *Think It Through* mystery is illustrated in this excerpt from the opening segment. There are two acceptable definitions of the problem, and both present the user with more choices, which in turn branch to further sections of the program, indicated by the letters at the far right. The "wrong" definition of the problem returns the user to the beginning.

From the flowchart, we began to develop the treatment. We approached this phase by using a three-column horizontal page, where the columns are labeled 1) video and text, 2) audio and 3) logic and viewer interaction. Writing the treatment in this format is extremely valuable because it forces you to write and *think* in interactive terms. For example, it lets you know if the viewer knows what to do when presented with a decision: Is the index on the screen? Has the narrator explained what's going on?[4]

Crown also recommends a three-column script to be sure that video, audio and viewer interactions line up properly. Storyboards can also be adapted to the nonlinear structure—telling how you got to this frame and where you're likely to be going next.

These specialized flowcharts, treatment and script formats simply highlight the writer's expanded role as program designer. It is a specialized form of writing, requiring a disciplined approach to organization and strict attention to details of the nonlinear structure.

Make Branching Meaningful

Branching can be an extremely effective teaching technique. But it can also make the learning experience more complex than necessary. As with any audio-visual technique or special effect, it should never be used because it is there but because content and teaching environment dictate its use. This is particularly important when branching involves decisions that lead to alternative scenarios—what to do next in treating a heart attack victim brought into the emergency room, for instance. The consequence of one or more alternative scenarios may be that the patient dies. The pay-off is not that the patient is lost but how the sequence can be analyzed by the student physician and what is learned as a result.

CONCLUSION: INTERACTIVE VIDEO—NOTHING NEW

As pointed out at the beginning of this chapter, interactive video is nothing new. Perhaps the greatest danger in the current enthusiasm for interactive video is that it is coming to mean only computer-assisted video learning. Other forms of interaction still have a place. Indeed, there may come a project when the best solution to the learning problem is to have students trace shapes or enter data on acetate placed over the screen. After all, that's what brought "Winky" to life.

---

[4]Peter Crown, "Going Interactive: Pointers from a Pioneering Producer," *Videography* (January 1982), p. 27.

12

Careers in Nonbroadcast Television: Three Interviews

In this chapter, four successful writers talk about their work in the three major areas of nonbroadcast television—education, medicine and business. Their comments illustrate varied aspects of the scriptwriting process: understanding the audience, setting and meeting objectives, conducting research and collaborating with content experts and production staff. The writers also discuss their writing habits and preferences and the backgrounds that brought them to nonbroadcast television.

THE EDUCATION WRITER:
VIDEO DISCS AND THE HEARING IMPAIRED

As a staff writer in the University of Nebraska's Educational Media Production Project for the Hearing Impaired, Casey Stone developed scripts targeted to a very specific audience: hearing-impaired children and their parents. Casey's writing assignments within this project, funded by the Office of Special Education, resulted in pioneering work in adapting video disc technology to the educational needs of this unique audience and have included other media as well. She also did freelance writing, including *Producing Interactive Discs*, a 3-M manual, and numerous articles for professional education journals. Since this interview, Casey has enrolled at Pennsylvania State University for a Ph.D. in instructional systems design and continues freelance writing.

I began by asking about the video disc portion of the project.

CASEY STONE: We first got started in January of 1979, when the technology was quite new. The Bureau of Education for the Handicapped, forerunner of the Office of Special Education, wanted to discover how video disc technology could be used to improve or enhance the education of the hearing impaired. Was the video disc something they should pay attention to? Did it offer long-term potential? So our role was to develop and evaluate experimental video discs for different age levels and for varied content areas. During the course of the project, we developed materials for use on the elementary, junior high and high school levels. We were also exploring varying levels of interactivity. We even looked at the needs of the parents of pre-school hearing-impaired children and developed materials that could be tested with parents in the home.

BILL VAN NOSTRAN: What type of programs have been produced for video disc?

CASEY STONE: Initially, nine programs were produced. Not all were interactive. In one, we took a previously developed video disc by Nebraska ETV and added closed captions. Closed captioning is a process whereby captions can be invisibly encoded onto television programs. One of the things we wanted to test was whether captioning would work on video discs. If it did, the same disc could be used with both deaf and hearing audiences. But first, we had to see whether there would be any interference with the encoded video disc signals.

Another linear program was targeted at teachers, administrators and others in the education of the hearing impaired—simply to familiarize them with the video disc and what it could do.

Programming aimed at people with normal hearing included "Words in Motion," which helped teach finger spelling, and "Language and Learning in the Home," teaching parents of pre-schoolers how to develop language skills with their hearing-impaired children.

BILL VAN NOSTRAN: What about programming aimed at the hearing-impaired kids?

CASEY STONE: For the junior high school level, we developed and tested a classroom geography lesson on Israel. Then we had a high school English literature lesson, "By Yourself," which featured a Ray Bradbury short story, two poems, a song and a glossary of more difficult words on a single disc.

BILL VAN NOSTRAN: How did you tell the Bradbury short story? Was it captioned?

CASEY STONE: It was captioned—almost every program was captioned and also had a sound track. The exception is "Words in Motion"—which taught finger spelling to adults. That had no sound track because we didn't want people to turn on the audio channel to discover what was being said.

BILL VAN NOSTRAN: So, back to the Bradbury story—was the story already on film and you added the captions?

CASEY STONE: No, we adapted it as a screenplay and filmed it ourselves. One of the major problems hearing-impaired children have is in reading. Learning language is extremely difficult for them. When most deaf children start school, they're lucky if they have a vocabulary of 40 or

50 words. There are lots of sentence structures that they have no contact with. They find it difficult to read and understand passive sentences, for instance. Also, what happens is that in order to encourage the children to read, the teachers rewrite literature down to the students' level. That gets them into a cycle of never learning anything more difficult because it's always being watered down to the same level.

On this disc, we tried using the visual capacity of the video disc to augment the literature. The visuals would carry enough content that even if the kids didn't understand every sentence or every word, they'd still get the meaning. So every word Bradbury wrote is there—but much of the information is being carried by watching. They are reading to augment what they're seeing.

BILL VAN NOSTRAN: You were in the middle of describing the range of projects before I side-tracked us.

CASEY STONE: The last two in the original series were the most interactive, using a microcomputer/video disc interface. We call it the *Think It Through* series. It evolved from another learning need we felt should be addressed. Hearing-impaired children live in such a structured environment, very often they don't have to think through a problem themselves. At home it's simpler for parents just to say: "Go do this." So we used the disc to establish a situation where the children first have to define the problem, and, based on the definition they've chosen, they are given a list of possible solutions from which they have to hypothesize which solution will work. Then they follow through to try and solve the problem through deduction.

We tried to simulate real-life problem solving where there's often more than one solution. Some approaches may be quicker than others, but that doesn't make them more correct. We're trying to get away from the idea of one right answer with everything else the wrong answer. Real life isn't that black and white.

BILL VAN NOSTRAN: What was the essence of the problems?

CASEY STONE: One is a mystery involving missing food coloring in a Mom and Pop grocery store. The child has to figure out what happened to it. We also built an authority figure into the script—Mr. Jones, the store owner. Lots of deaf kids depend on the teacher or mother for the right answer. So we built in the character who is always there, and the program permits the kids to ask: "Is this right? What are the choices?" They can ask Mr. Jones; but more often than not, Mr. Jones says, "I don't know." We're trying to wean them away from always going to an adult to get an answer.

The second problem is a story about a little deaf girl going to visit a friend. This is the first time she's taken a bus alone. Her mother gives her directions, but she gets on the bus and fails to pay attention. She loses track of where she is. She looks up and doesn't know if she's gone past her stop. She gets off the bus, not knowing what to do next. The kids have to work through possible solutions to her dilemma.

BILL VAN NOSTRAN: What are you working on currently?

CASEY STONE: I recently completed a program on voting for the high school level, which involved a video tape, two filmstrips and a workbook. One filmstrip explains what you have to do to register and vote. That's followed by a video dramatization of a young deaf man going through the process for the first time. The mode of communication is largely sign language, but all the sign language is captioned because there are some viewers who are not proficient at reading sign language. Some schools don't even encourage it. In addition, when this man goes to vote, the person in the registration office doesn't know sign language so she simply speaks to him; at times they write notes back and forth.

BILL VAN NOSTRAN: How have you developed a sensitivity to the special requirements of this audience?

CASEY STONE: It's an ongoing process. There's a good body of research regarding the special problems of the hearing impaired—and I've made it a point to read a fair amount of that literature. We have other people within the project to draw upon. During the initial federal contract, others did extensive work on language development among hearing-impaired children. From that, we learned a lot about semantics and syntax for the target population—what age you can start putting direct discourse in, for example; what level you can start using the passive voice, things like that.

Then, depending on the nature of the project, we may need to bring in content specialists or go out and do independent research. When we did the finger spelling video disc, for example, we brought in people who are experts at teaching sign language. And, of course, just working with children, you find out where they are and what they are able to do.

BILL VAN NOSTRAN: Getting back to the actual program design and scripting process, how did you acquire the skills for doing interactive writing?

CASEY STONE: The first things I started out writing were very linear. The instructional designer I worked with had background in television but had never done anything interactive. So we just dived in and learned as we went along. We attended conferences to learn from people in the field, but after reading and working out some problems ourselves, we found we knew about as much as those giving seminars at the conferences.

One technique I'm a big advocate of when it comes to doing interactive programming is flowcharting. You have a lot of elements to keep track of—not only the different video disc branches, but also pages of print. You have to account for codes on disc players. You really have to be able to illustrate to the producer/director and the software programmer precisely how everything fits together. It takes more to communicate and account for all those things on paper than is possible in a standard video script format. That's when flowcharting becomes invaluable.

BILL VAN NOSTRAN: How do you determine whether a flowchart is necessary?

CASEY STONE: I would use a flowchart anytime I had interactive material. I got started on the first *Think It Through* program and just started writing one page after another, and I was fine the first day. Then the next day I came back to try and pick it up. Suddenly the branches became totally confusing, and I was lost. That's when I did my first flowchart and I found it helped solidify the overall structure. When you're dealing with something highly interactive, it's dangerous to make it up as you go along. It's good to have the whole pattern very well thought out. The flowchart I make up initially may not look like the one I eventually turn in for production because things change as you write—you modify as you go along.

BILL VAN NOSTRAN: A theme throughout this book is the collaborative process of creating television programming. In doing interactive video discs, you deal with yet another collaborator—the software programmer. Tell me about your approach to collaboration.

CASEY STONE: The relationship's very similar to working with the producer. I like to talk with the programmer fairly early on before you get locked into things. You should make certain that what you have in mind as interaction or branching is feasible. Make sure you're not going to have more information in the computer than the computer is capable of controlling. We also prepare a special script for the programmer more like the flowchart than a production script. This is used to communicate how various program elements fit together from one point to the next. It's all got to be spelled out quite specifically and logically. You can't assume anything.

BILL VAN NOSTRAN: I'd like to shift gears and ask when and how you first became interested in writing?

CASEY STONE: I've always been interested in writing. I remember when I was eight years old complaining to my mother that I had nothing to do. My mother wrote instructional material for the Lutheran Church, and she said: "Well, why don't you write a play?" So I sat down and started writing. I don't know that I ever finished the play but that's how far back I can remember wanting to write.

After graduating as a philosophy major, I worked for a publishing company as a cost estimator for a year. I really didn't take to publishing. Part of it was the first-job syndrome, and part of it was the tremendous pressure. Further, in my job, I was associated entirely with the *cost* of the book, not the quality of it.

I tried teaching, and then I worked as a secretary in the Office of Communications for the Lutheran Church in America in New York City. I learned a lot about TV, radio, film and newspapers. When my husband decided to get an MFA in theater at Nebraska, we moved here, and I was in the job market again.

The first thing I was offered was as secretary for the associate director of this project. A year later the video disc project was added. At first, they were looking for someone with experience with the hearing impaired, who had experience writing for television, who had experience programming computers—several other requirements—and willing to live in Nebraska, all for not that big a salary. It became apparent the person they were looking for didn't exist. I applied for the job since I'd learned sign language, knew what the project was all about and had some background in writing and media. I got lucky. I was in the right place at the right time.

BILL VAN NOSTRAN: What preferences do you have toward writing habits? Do you have a particular time of day you like to write? Do you prefer writing in the office or at home?

CASEY STONE: Since we're required to be in the office 40 hours a week, most of my project writing is done in the office. I do like to isolate myself when writing and cut out all other intrusions. I like to work for extended periods of time. I like doing freelance work late in the evening. I tend to go home, do things around the house, run errands, then maybe get writing at about nine and go late.

BILL VAN NOSTRAN: Do you compose in longhand or at the typewriter?

CASEY STONE: I generally write in longhand. It's easier for me to cross out and move things around. At the typewriter, I have more difficulty doing that.

BILL VAN NOSTRAN: Tell me about some of the freelance projects you've worked on.

CASEY STONE: I did a project for the Florida Health and Rehabilitation Services and University of Florida. They were putting all their training materials on video disc. The University of Nebraska was contracted for production, and they hired me as writer. The first program was a primer on the disc itself—what its capabilities are; how to operate it; what to do if they had a problem. In a similar vein, I did a manual for 3-M to accompany a video disc on instructional design and authoring for the disc.

BILL VAN NOSTRAN: How do you handle the freelance work on top of the ongoing project writing?

CASEY STONE: Sometimes I'll make tradeoffs. If, for instance, I meet with a producer on a freelance project from three to five—then I'll come back to the office and make up for that time. There are times when I ask: "What have I gotten into?" But I really enjoy working on programs outside of the hearing impaired project. You have different audiences, different types of production considerations, *and* I don't have to worry about *language* restraints!

BILL VAN NOSTRAN: Your work in the project seems to have encompassed many styles—from narration to dramatic vignettes to mime. How do you arrive at those decisions, and what special writing skills are required?

CASEY STONE: The actual decision as to whether something will be narration or drama is made in the design stage. That's based on an analysis of what we're trying to do and how we can best get it across. You work out your objectives, look at your audience and tie the two together. With the hearing impaired, you need action on the screen. The only way a deaf person is going to understand what's happening is through dramatic action or mime. As far as the actual writing, once I get the overall structure and plan, then these little people sit in my head and talk, and I transcribe what they say.

BILL VAN NOSTRAN: What advice would you give to someone who read this and said, "Gee, what you do sounds like something I'd like to do. How can I get into this field?"

CASEY STONE: That's difficult to answer since I kind of fell into it. Personally, I think a liberal arts background is important. I find I need to know so many little things that a broad background is needed. I've never been in a program that's supposed to turn out writers so I don't really know how helpful that can be. Just write. Write as much as you can. That's the best way to learn to write—just doing it. Then be self-critical and objective about what you've written.

MEDICAL WRITERS:
CONTINUING EDUCATION FOR PHYSICIANS

The Network for Continuing Medical Education (NCME) has provided continuing physician education through a subscription video cassette service since 1965. As a division of Visual Information Systems, a Manhattan production company specializing in medical programming, NCME offers continuing medical education programs for credit to accredited medical schools and hospitals. Approximately 23 hours of programming are conceived, developed and produced by NCME staff writers and directors each year. Some are in-depth treatments of specific medical topics. They include training and testing techniques, and carry the highest level (Category I) of continuing education credits. Recent NCME releases run the therapeutic gamut from "The Clinical Spectrum of Vasculitis" to "Adolescent Psychiatry." Visual Information Systems also operates a news/feature radio network called Physician's Radio Network (PRN).

Program content is developed in conjunction with medical schools, NCME's advisory board and physicians who are recognized specialists on the subject at hand and who may also serve as on-camera presenters. To learn more about the writer's role in such projects, I spoke with Uli Monaco, director of programming at NCME, and Lois Gaeta, one of four staff writers/co-producers. I asked Uli Monaco to provide an overview of the program development process at NCME.

ULI MONACO: In the first quarter of each year we mail a questionnaire to the 700-plus Directors of Medical Education (DMEs) in subscribing hospitals. The form lists the programs—both hour-long Category I telecourses and short 17-minute subjects—that have been produced during the current year. We ask the DMEs to document additional educational needs of staff physicians. These survey results are compiled and sent out to 12 medical advisors, who are leading family physicians and specialists attuned to the continuing educational needs of our physician audience.

The advisors do a preliminary voting on topics for the upcoming year. The annual programming process goes like this: During June of each year, the four NCME writers, three directors and two associate producers meet with David Barnhizer, our vice president for programming and production, to discuss the 12 hour-long telecourses and 33 short subject programs that have been selected. Assignments are made, and the production process is put into action. The advisors are also asked to recommend physician/faculty presenters who have proven their teaching ability and are expected to have good on-camera presence.

LOIS GAETA: We try to work with the known authority in each field. But, increasingly, we've had good success in working with the up-and-coming physician/teachers; people who are still fresh in their approach, yet who can give competent clinically and scientifically based presentations.

ULI MONACO: We often talk to several people before we find someone who we think meets our criteria and who can also fit the project into their schedule.

LOIS GAETA: Between our initial telephone call and the first research meeting, we send the physician a letter that includes an NCME catalog, some sample Category I telecourse workbooks or TV guides from short shows. The letter details what they are in for. Increasingly, I'm documenting in advance how much time it will take, what each phase of the process will require, etc.

ULI MONACO: The first meeting with the presenter takes about three hours, more for a Category I program. Whenever possible, the director assigned to the project also attends. We discuss the general goals, the time frame within which we're working and then proceed with the interview. Most of our writers record the interview on audio cassette, which is transcribed for use in writing a rough draft of the script.

BILL VAN NOSTRAN: How do you go about preparing for an interview?

LOIS GAETA: First, we go to the library and bone up on the subject. We have a good supply of medical textbooks and a file of all of the major medical magazines. In addition, we have the resource files of the Physicians Radio Network to draw upon. For example, when I was researching the material for a Category I telecourse on shock, all of the information I needed—including the current controversies—was in the PRN shock file. As the interview was progressing, I could almost predict the topic the presenter was going to discuss next.

BILL VAN NOSTRAN: What are you looking for from the initial interview?

ULI MONACO: We listen to how clearly the physician states educational objectives. Do they have a definite idea of what they want to teach? Are they prepared for the interview?

LOIS GAETA: A couple of presenters have handed us outlines when we have walked into the room. "I just put a few thoughts on paper," they say. This shows they've really thought about what they want to communicate. Generally those few thoughts become the structure for the entire telecourse.

ULI MONACO: We must also evaluate how well they can convey their information on TV. We keep stressing that the faculty members are physicians, not actors. But they still have to have presence. If not, viewing physicians lose patience very quickly, and we lose our audience.

BILL VAN NOSTRAN: Do your telecourse scripts follow a set format?

ULI MONACO: Pretty much. However, the style of each telecourse is dictated by the material that the presenter wants to teach as well as our decisions on the most effective way to get it across. We try to get the personality of the presenter into the script. Now and then we might interject a little humor or a personal vignette that the presenter has told us. In other words, we want the material to come from the physicians. It's their telecourse. We are there to help teach via the medium of video tape.

LOIS GAETA: Generally, the agenda of the first meeting goes like this: a description of the project and the details, a discussion of the four or five educational objectives and an agreement as to the form and content of the program.

ULI MONACO: During the meeting, we ask the physician if he or she has any available visuals, such as color slides of clinical or pathological findings.

LOIS GAETA: To write the rough draft of the script, we work with the transcript of the interview, as well as any papers the physician recommended. I always tell a physician that what he or she gives to me, I give back. Thus, the quality of the interview relates directly to the quality of the draft of the script that he or she will receive.

BILL VAN NOSTRAN: You not only write the script, but you've got to develop a complete training program with collateral print and testing vehicles, correct?

ULI MONACO: That's right. During that first meeting, we also discuss content for the telecourse workbook or TV guide material. In order for a program to qualify for Category I credit, we need to have a pre-quiz and post-telecourse quiz, plus additional study and suggested references.

LOIS GAETA: Recently, while developing a program on lung cancer, we ran a pre-telecourse quiz twice in previous telecourse workbooks. We used the results of the pre-telecourse quiz to develop the educational objectives and focus of the telecourse and selection of ancillary material. Now we're awaiting the results of the post-telecourse quiz. We want to learn if basing a telecourse on proven educational needs helps to improve the test results at the end of the viewing.

BILL VAN NOSTRAN: You are working, by and large, with experienced teachers. How do they feel about being scripted?

ULI MONACO: It is a challenge to convince many of them that scripts are the way to structure a video tape according to educational objectives. We often hear, "I've done this lecture a million times, and I really don't need a script. In fact, I don't even work well with a script."

LOIS GAETA: The director is always quick to point out that the video tape is going to be shot out of sequence and edited together much like a jigsaw puzzle. For example, all of the on-camera scenes are shot at once, then the voice-overs. The clinical exams are taped in one section and the slides in another. The physician is going to be in trouble if he thinks he can start at Scene 1 and speak straight through to Scene 27.

ULI MONACO: In the "bad old days," we used to work without scripts. We used to fit slides into a physician's lecture. But we found that we weren't teaching as effectively as we knew we could. We weren't getting enough out of the television medium, nor were we doing justice to the physician. The reason we fit so much material into these programs is because they *are* so well planned out, scene by scene. We put more information into 17 minutes than a lot of physicians believe we'll be able to do in an hour.

LOIS GAETA: Two scenes into the taping, even the most resistant physician realizes how necessary a script is. Invariably, physicians who at first give us the biggest argument about developing a script will say at the end: "You were right."

BILL VAN NOSTRAN: You mentioned that the director often accompanies you on an interview. What is your relationship with the director?

ULI MONACO: Our responsibilities as co-producers dovetail. We, the writer/co-producers, invite the physician to do the program and set up the initial interview. Then we are fairly much in charge of running the preliminary meeting during which we get the material. The director's role is to help us decide whether or not the physician will come across well on video tape, to explore the visual possibilities and, if location shooting is indicated, to check out the locations.

BILL VAN NOSTRAN: Have you ever found yourself in the position of interviewing a physician, then deciding that it's not in everyone's best interest to go forward with the project?

LOIS GAETA: That's where the director's experience is useful. Between the two of us we can generally spot a physician who won't be effective on video tape. The physician may have a monotone voice or some mannerism that will grate on the audience. In those cases, we might close the interview by saying that we would like to speak with the medical advisory board about the project before proceeding.

ULI MONACO: It's a sensitive area, not continuing with a physician. However, sometimes, after the fact, we regret not taking a stand early on and changing topics or seeking other presenters.

LOIS GAETA: For instance, recently, a world famous lecturer did so poorly during video taping that we had to hire a professional announcer to do a voice-over for several sections. I must confess that because of tight schedules, a director didn't go on the initial interview with me. I came back to the office with a great deal of concern about the physician's TV presence. However, since he is *the* authority on his subject, we decided to play the long shot. In this case we lost.

BILL VAN NOSTRAN: Let's get back to the relationship with the director.

ULI MONACO: After a first draft script has been written, the writer and director work on developing visuals. At this point, the director and assistant director begin to take over the bulk of the responsibility of the video tape from the writer.

BILL VAN NOSTRAN: What happens when writer and director have differences of opinion on how to present a subject?

ULI MONACO: If creative professionals don't disagree upon occasion, one of us isn't doing our job. Each of us has strengths and weaknesses, and we learn to work productively together. For example, the writers have more medical background than the directors, while directors have more practical production experience.

BILL VAN NOSTRAN: Do you ever find yourself working with content that fights the medium of television?

ULI MONACO: Often. That's why we try to develop clinical programs, not theoretical ones. In that initial interview you'll talk a great deal about the ultimate visualization of the program. If you do a program on X-rays, for example, obviously you're going to talk a lot about what it's going to look like. On others, the directors simply listen and try to get some idea of what it's going to be about so they can start thinking about it. My Category I telecourse on hydrogen ions was a big challenge. The solution was to develop patient cases—then move from the patient material to the physics of what was happening. We also did some simple animation—because we have limited budgets, the animation has to be simple. We sometimes hear the complaint that a program is too much of a lecture, too many talking heads. We constantly battle this problem when a program is nonvisual.

LOIS GAETA: Sometimes it's hard to get a grip on the subject matter and cast the content in the television format. I did a program once on the five phases of acute myocardial infarction (heart attack). The research interview was four hours, and I didn't have any idea of a format. After I thought about it a great deal, I decided: "Why not give a *doctor* a heart attack and build the presentation around that?" So we created a fictional physician and made him high risk. The viewing physicians saw him having the heart attack and followed him through to where he returned to practice. That story line provided a focus for all material and built audience involvement since the "patient" was a doctor.

BILL VAN NOSTRAN: How do you know what level to aim your program at? Do you find yourself talking down to some specialists and over the heads of others?

LOIS GAETA: We've had that criticism, and we are being conscientious in correcting it. In recent interviews, I've asked the physician to target the material to a fairly sophisticated audience, one that is accustomed to reading the *New England Journal of Medicine* and *Lancet.*

BILL VAN NOSTRAN: Do you enjoy the whole process of taking complex medical subjects and shaping them into a viewing experience?

LOIS GAETA: We have a chance to be creative. Since this is clinical medicine, we hope that the creative doesn't stand out and dominate content. But each program has its own unique challenges. You have to let the material dictate the final form.

BILL VAN NOSTRAN: How do you find working with physicians?

ULI MONACO: It depends on the physician. Physicians are people, like the rest of us. As a group, the ones we work with tend to be very good teachers and well respected professionals. They are usually captivated by the idea of working on video tape.

LOIS GAETA: I suspect that the way they work with us reflects the way they approach teaching and writing projects in general. We have to adapt our schedules to suit the physicians' schedules. For example, a Category I telecourse script on shock needed a pretty thorough rewrite. But the physician was so busy traveling and lecturing—I used to say "he's on the Shock Circuit"—that he never had time to sit down and work on it. So to circumvent that—you know, if you've been in the business for a while, you see problems coming—I asked his secretary about his schedule. Well, it just so happened he was going to be in New Orleans at the same time I was going to be there on a different interview. So what I did was grab him for three hours before he gave a lecture. We were able to develop such a polished final script that I didn't need to go to the video taping (a budget consideration). The director reported that there were only a few word changes during the taping.

BILL VAN NOSTRAN: Summarize your own personal backgrounds. How did you both get into writing medical television programming? Also, do you have a science background?

ULI MONACO: I started out as a writer. I wrote a lot of fiction. And I worked in public relations. Then someone offered me a job doing medical writing for lay people, which seemed simple enough. I did that for a time and then moved into medical writing for physicians.

LOIS GAETA: I did take chemistry at college, but my background wasn't scientific. I studied television writing and then went to J. Walter Thompson as a TV-radio copy writer for over-the-counter products. Then I was with a pharmaceutical company for several years. NCME gives me a chance to combine television and the medical.

BILL VAN NOSTRAN: Is a scientific background desirable, or should one become a writer first and worry about learning the medical end second?

LOIS GAETA: I think you get at the end by various routes. If you're going to be a professional writer, you have to be able to write, and you have to decide whether you're going to write cosmetics or fashion or medicine. I decided, finally, that it was going to be medicine.

ULI MONACO: Some medical writers started out with medicine, although not many. Medical journalism courses are available and helpful. But, with few exceptions, I think you start out with the writing interest before the medical.

BILL VAN NOSTRAN: How did you learn to write instructional objectives?

LOIS GAETA: We studied the guidebooks and the articles written on the subject. Writing educational objectives simply takes having a clear idea of the practical outcomes of the program.

BILL VAN NOSTRAN: Do you both write here in the office?

ULI MONACO: Yes.

BILL VAN NOSTRAN: And how is your day normally organized?

ULI MONACO: One of the pleasant things about this job is that one's day is not normally organized the same way every day.

LOIS GAETA: What I usually do the night before, and this sounds like something right out of the time management text books, but I make a list of things to do the following day.

ULI MONACO: Yes, I do that too...

LOIS GAETA: If I come in here, and someone brings up a problem or I get a phone call or something—I can get completely sidetracked. I like to write in long blocks of time. I require absolute solitude to write. I can't write with anybody in the room. And, if there's an overload of work, I work weekends. We all do. I'll bring it home and write at home. But I like writing long hours.

ULI MONACO: I like to have time to write, too. That's the best way to do it. I'm able to concentrate even with an office mate. And I can work during normal office hours. We have had writers who couldn't write during the day. They would only write after midnight. That's a problem for a staff member because you have to be in the office. People come by and ask questions about last month's release or next week's taping or a hundred other things.

BILL VAN NOSTRAN: Do you write in longhand or on typewriters?

ULI MONACO: I write on a typewriter.

LOIS GAETA: I've been training myself to compose on the typewriter as preparation for the arrival of the word processor.

BILL VAN NOSTRAN: Do you ever suffer from writer's block?

ULI MONACO: Of course. Some of these subjects are tough to move right into. But you have a schedule that you have to meet. We just keep at it and keep at it, and finally material falls into place. After a while, it becomes easier. Each of us has to turn out three 1-hour programs and eight 17-minute programs each year. It is a lot of work, but it's not an unheard of amount.

BILL VAN NOSTRAN: What happens when you have done the same types of projects year in and year out?

ULI MONACO: By then, special projects or variations on our assignments have come up. We are currently doing video tapes for dentists and are working with the American Dental Association on developing them. Because of the home video market and the growing interest in audio-visual materials on everyone's part, we feel as if we are where it's at!

THE FREELANCE WRITER IN THE CORPORATE WORLD

Bill Van Nostran develops, writes and produces video programming for Fortune 500 clients. His background includes extensive staff experience in organizational communications for major corporations as well as the U.S. Air Force. In the following "interview," Bill responds to his own questions about the role of the scriptwriter in a corporate TV environment.

Q: You've been both a staff writer and a freelancer. How would you compare the two?
A: Well, one comes complete with a paycheck every two weeks, while the other one offers the excitement of cash flow problems...
Q: Seriously now...
A: In terms of the actual writing process, there's really no difference. Freelancers and staff writers alike must go through the identical process of getting a handle on audience, objectives and content. In the research phase, the staff writer may have it easier with more access to in-house resources and a greater insight into the dynamics of the organization. The freelancer, however, usually has more varied experiences to draw upon.

Probably the major difference is that the freelancer has more options in terms of subject matter. Certainly, I enjoy the variety in freelance assignments. You know—working up a pharmaceutical sales presentation one week, then an EEO training program the next, for two different organizations. That's very stimulating.

Q: Aside from the steady paycheck, what are the advantages of a staff job?
A: I think a staff position is the ideal place to learn and refine your craft. In a staff job, generally, your assignments come in on a fairly regular basis. You have good access to in-house resources. And, in larger departments, you rub shoulders daily with colleagues coping with similar problems. I'd also say that the environment of most staff jobs is more forgiving. By that I mean, you risk less by experimenting with the medium and trying things out. You can't make a career of that obviously—but when you do push the medium or a program format to a creative threshold for that organization, you risk less. As a freelancer, one less than completely satsifying experience with a client and you may never be called in again.

Q: Are you saying that a freelancer should play it safer—"closer to the vest?"
A: No—not by a long shot. In fact, if anything, my own work as a freelancer has become bolder than when I wrote as a staff member. But I think that comes from experience and the confidence of having done scripts for years—often several on similar subjects. You also need enough

experience to size up which way the "corporate wind" is blowing on any given project. A writer has to sense the political, financial and logistical parameters of each assignment. Those tell you, to a large extent, how far you can move a client in the direction you wish to go. Now, the freelancer often has more leverage than the staff person. It's that old outside consultant mystique.

Q: Why are you so concerned about "moving a client" in a certain direction?

A: Let me try and explain it this way. In the corporate setting, television should be reserved for high priority communications/training applications. You shouldn't be using television for messages that can be conveyed just as well through a simple memo, or a training program that can be done effectively and efficiently with audio cassettes and a workbook. It seems to me that if you've selected the medium for the right reasons, you should wind up with a *high impact communication*. Yet that rarely is the end result. All too often, corporate programming is bland, predictable and uninvolving. This happens for a variety of reasons. Often, it's the corporate imperative to play it safe. But just as often, programs are unimaginative and lack impact because the writing is unimaginative. The challenge is to find a format, style or treatment of a subject which is simultaneously appropriate to the organization *and* engaging for the audience. To really involve an audience, I think you have to do the unexpected. That's what I mean by pushing the medium to its limit within an organization.

Q: What about lifestyle differences between the freelancer and staff person?

A: I joke about the financial pressures of freelancing, but there's more to it than that. The freelancer's whole lifestyle is different from a staff person's. A freelancer has to be disciplined and highly motivated. (I personally find fear of starvation a superb motivator.) If you write at home, as many freelancers do, you have to develop a mental mind-set which says "Now I'm at work," and not let yourself get distracted. The freelancer also does not enjoy the camaraderie that staff people get from colleagues. Staff writers invariably seem to think the freelancer's lot is better. In reality, freelancing brings its own set of problems that may prove more frustrating to some than the problems of a staff job. As a freelancer, for instance, you spend a lot of time and energy running a business. That cuts into writing time.

Q: How have things changed in corporate television since you began?

A: My first real corporate television writing dates back to the early 1970s. That was an interesting period because the video cassette player was making corporate television networks much more feasible for many organizations, but there were far fewer opportunities for writers. In those days, the field was dominated to a large extent by audio-visual mavens—people who were hardware oriented and wanted to build big in-house facilities. In many cases, it was only after companies had invested in equipment that anyone started to think: "Say, we really should have some people who can help us use this equipment to communicate and instruct—some people with good research, conceptual and writing skills."

I think the corporate television community has a greater appreciation today of the role of the writer in the production process and the necessity for having a good script in crafting a good program. For that reason, there's a lot more work for both staff writers and freelancers than there was a decade ago. I still find it amusing, however, to see employment ads for jobs in corporate television that read: "Wanted—Producer/Director/Writer." Give me a break! There's a good reason why those three functions should be performed by different people. Each ought to represent an "advocate" position toward the project from a different perspective. When it's all one person, there's no one to "argue" with. The give and take of collaboration is lost. Usually the project suffers because very few people can perform all three functions equally well.

Q: Let me shift directions and ask some questions about your writing habits. First—do you compose longhand or on a typewriter?

A: Well, for about 12 years, every first draft was in longhand. Then I did a revision on the typewriter, working from the first draft. Then I would do final corrections in pencil and hand the manuscript over for typing. However, all this has changed since Van Nostran Associates purchased an industrial grade word processor. It's revolutionized my approach to generating a first draft. I now use the word processor to compose on. The screen has become an "electronic legal pad." I find the touch of the electronic keyboard less mechanical than the typewriter. Also, you don't worry about typos since they're so easily corrected. You can move words and sentences around, make deletions, etc. Only once you have a first draft and store it on a floppy disk—you have a manuscript. I print it out, then make corrections on the manuscript. From then on, it's a simple matter of continually updating the disk with rewrites.

Q: So you've entered the electronic scriptwriting age?

A: Yes—although we're still learning the full range of capabilities of our equipment. We've barely scratched the surface. You can, for example, enter basic research for a project onto a disk—then incorporate material into a first draft without having to retype it. Eventually, we'll get a modem which will put us in touch with the growing information retrieval community over telephone lines. Someday, we'll probably transmit scripts to distant clients electronically rather than through the mails. We'll also probably do a lot of research electronically from the home rather than going to the library. I think there's been a tendency in the corporate world to view the word processor as a secretarial tool. In many fields, that's appropriate. But in ad agencies, public relations agencies and communication departments where business writers crank out tons of copy, the word processor should be thought of as an electronic composition tool first.

Q: What advice would you give someone contemplating a career in corporate television?

A: You mean, students—college students interested in this field?

Q: That's right.

A: If they're anything like I was in college they won't take this advice anyway—but I think the broader a writer's education, the better. I would advise staying away from journalism courses. I think they teach formula writing rather than conceptual writing. Go for courses in English, theater and media departments. Take courses that sharpen your critical abilities. The only reason for a writer to go to college is to learn to think. If you can *think* with clarity, you should eventually be able to write with clarity. I think a television writer should take a lot of theater courses. First off, it develops an ear for the spoken word, which is what television writing is all about. And such things as character development and dramatic conflict come only through exposure to theater.

I don't think any course of study is superfluous for a writer. In my own case, I wish I'd studied economics and taken some marketing and management courses. Art history and aesthetics are great subjects for anyone who wants to write visual material. Of course, I'm assuming these people will study film history, TV and film production and communications theory. Photography and publication design are also very good practical training to have. There are still more jobs in print than there are in television in corporations.

One other point—sooner or later, you must do some apprenticing in the professional video production world. It's the only way to learn how programming really gets produced. And a writer must know television production to write for this medium.

Q: How do you view the television writer's function in the corporate context?

A: It's quite simple, really. You are management's "mouthpiece." That sounds terribly subservient, and some people have an innate resistance to such a self-image. But to be a professional writer in the corporate arena, you have to accept the fact that television is a management tool and your function is to help management use that tool effectively.

Now that doesn't mean you have to be a "yes" man in the organization. But your recommendations should always stem from a *studied* understanding of the business and corporate environment in which you're operating. If you work in the oil industry—become a student of the oil industry. At the same time, study your own organization. Soak up information over drinks at corporate functions. Attend meetings just to learn what's going on. Be nosey—take field trips with sales reps. Visit manufacturing plants. Sit in on showings of your own video programming. The more confident you are with the dynamics of your own organization and its business, the more valid your recommendations will be, and the more weight they will carry.

Q: Isn't there a lot of mundane material in the world of corporate TV?

A: I don't buy that. I think there's a lot of insipid writing in the corporate world. My philosophy is that there's no such thing as a boring subject— there's only boring writing. Now, that doesn't mean that certain kinds of material aren't better suited to treatment in a medium other than television. But that is a problem of media selection and application.

Q: How do you see the field evolving over the next several years?

A: I think there will be more and more opportunities for people to specialize in corporate television writing. I also think there will be a gradual blurring of the distinction between writing nonbroadcast material and writing cable and traditional broadcast material. So there will be more opportunities for truly talented writers to work with subject matter and formats that go beyond sit-coms and one-hour action-adventure shows. Not that there haven't been some beautifully written sit-coms. But all that work is centered around the Hollywood establishment and probably always will be. That's where the money is. I don't think any writer will get rich writing corporate television programming. But if you're good at it and enjoy it, you can make a reasonable living writing corporate programs. If you really enjoy writing, it's a privilege to do what you enjoy and get paid for it.

Appendix A:
The Business of Nonbroadcast Scriptwriting

In broadcast television, the Writers Guild of America negotiates and administers minimum basic agreements with major film producers and broadcasting networks and stations, covering theatrical and television films, live and taped television, documentary film and radio. The nonbroadcast market, by contrast, is nonunionized. The diversity of employers and the specialized nature of nonbroadcast writing create an open market in which writers and would-be writers negotiate a salary or freelance fee on their own.

STAFF WRITING JOBS

Staff jobs in the corporate, educational and medical markets are limited. The International Television Association (ITVA) conducts an annual salary survey of its membership. In 1982, 1,348 members responded to the salary survey; only 2.3%—about 31 members—described their jobs as "Writer." It's likely many more staff people write scripts as part of their duties as producer or director or media specialist or any one of several hyphenated job descriptions such as producer-director or producer-director-writer. Despite the growth of nonbroadcast television and greater recognition of the writer's role in nonbroadcast productions, staff jobs for writers are not in great abundance. Writers willing to write for print and other audio-visual media as well as television or scriptwriters with instructional design or training capabilities will find more opportunities for full-time staff employment than someone seeking a staff job exclusively as a nonbroadcast TV writer.

According to the 1982 ITVA salary survey, writers' salaries ranged from $13,800 to over $30,000. Although one writer reported an income of $70,000, the midpoint for all writers was $20,500. While this survey does not distinguish between salaried and freelance writers, the 1981 survey by a short-lived publication, *Videowriter*, did do so. In that survey, staff salaries ranged from a low of $10,000 to a high of $55,000 with a mean salary of $23,400. From these two surveys, one can surmise that in 1981-1982, an average salary for a staff video writer was in the mid-twenties. A newcomer trying to break into the field could expect considerably less, while a seasoned writer should be earning $30,000 or more.

FREELANCE WRITING

As you might expect, a freelance nonbroadcast writer has the *potential* for greater earnings than salaried counterparts. Obviously, the more productive and prolific a writer, the more opportunity to capitalize on freelance opportunities. The *Videowriter* survey confirms this notion. The mean freelance salary came to $33,900. The highest salary topped $100,000!

Freelance nonbroadcast writers have various ways of calculating fees. Some use a daily or hourly rate. Others charge by calculating a fee per minute of product. If a writer's fee is $200 per screen minute, a 20-minute program would be billed at $4,000. Another method of pricing involves a flat fee based on the nature of each individual project. This allows the writer to take into account such factors as demand for fast turnaround or a high visibility project. A rule of thumb from film production puts the writer's fee at about 10% of the total budget for the project. Thus, a project budgeted at $75,000 should include about $7,500 for scriptwriting. (This 10% rule is not valid when production costs are absorbed as operating expenses of an in-house facility—quite common in today's nonbroadcast environment.)

Most freelance writers make arrangements to bill clients in stages as work progresses. Typically, one-third of the fee is billed early in a project, another third when a first draft script is delivered and the final third on completion of all rewrites. When working on large-scale, protracted projects, the writer should nail down terms and conditions through a formal contract or, at the very least, a letter of agreement.

Although freelance writers in the nonbroadcast field appear to earn more than their counterparts in staff jobs, they also have the additional expenses and time demands that running a small business entails—from postage and supplies to such major items as office space and equipment, travel and entertainment expenses, accounting and legal fees and the cost of insurance programs generally paid as benefits to the staff person.

Appendix B:
Professional Organizations

The following professional organizations provide useful contacts and services for their membership. Most of these organizations have local chapters that meet on a regular basis. In addition, the national organizations typically hold annual conferences, sponsor contests, publish newsletters and, in some cases, serve as a source of job leads. For more information, write the national office or contact a local chapter of the organization.

Don't overlook other industry trade groups as research sources for writing projects. All these groups serve as advocates for their industry and have current background information on file and free for the asking.

INTERNATIONAL TELEVISION ASSOCIATION (ITVA)
International Offices
136 Sherman Avenue
Berkeley Heights, NJ 07922

This is an association of video professionals working primarily in nonbroadcast televison. There are local chapters throughout the United States and Canada.

INTERNATIONAL ASSOCIATION OF BUSINESS
COMMUNICATORS (IABC)
Suite 928
870 Market Street
San Francisco, CA 94102

This organization centers on business and organizational communication, regardless of the medium. Although traditionally the membership consisted of print-oriented people, recent years have seen more emphasis on audio-visual media used to achieve business communication objectives.

NATIONAL AUDIO-VISUAL ASSOCIATION (NAVA)
3150 Spring Street
Fairfax, VA 22031

Although equipment supplier/dealer oriented, the group is quite active in the total audio-visual arena.

AMERICAN SOCIETY FOR TRAINING AND DEVELOPMENT
INC. (ASTD)
Suite 305
600 Maryland Ave. S.W.
Washington, DC 20024

This group consists of organizational and industrial trainers who may use video, film and other audio-visual media to achieve training objectives.

PUBLIC RELATIONS SOCIETY OF AMERICA (PRSA)
845 Third Avenue
New York, NY 10022

For communicators involved in public relations and employee communications.

INFORMATION FILM PRODUCERS OF AMERICA (IFPA)
Suite 6
750 E. Colorado Blvd.
Pasadena, CA 91101

An association of film producers and sponsors working in the area of films (and video tape) with informational purposes.

AMERICAN FILM INSTITUTE
John F. Kennedy Center
Washington, DC 20566

Although the organization centers on the feature film industry, there are good reasons for becoming a member (such as *American Film* magazine), especially if you have an interest in using dramatic techniques in nonbroadcast programming.

Glossary

Actuality audio: Audio that is recorded on location to capture the sounds and ambience of an environment. Generally, this is unscripted audio used more as a sound effect than to convey content. Examples could include the sounds of an airport terminal, a hospital lobby or a manufacturing facility.

Camera directions: Television production terminology that describes the relationship between the camera and the object being shot. The television writer uses the following terms to describe the *distance* between camera and subject:

> LONG SHOT (LS)
> MEDIUM SHOT (MS)
> CLOSE UP (CU)
> EXTREME CLOSE UP (ECU)

To define *movement* of the camera in relation to the subject, the writer uses such terms as:

> PAN RIGHT/LEFT—A horizontal rotation of the camera on a fixed axis.
> TILT UP/DOWN—Vertical movement of the camera on a fixed axis.
> DOLLY—Physically moving the camera closer or farther from the subject.
> TRUCK—Physically moving the camera left or right on a horizontal plane, parallel to the subject.
> ZOOM IN/OUT—Changing the focal length of the lens to make the subject appear larger or smaller.

Character generator: An electronic method of adding text in the form of titles or supers to a video picture. Text is created on a typewriter-like keyboard, then electronically superimposed over another video image.

Cyclorama (cyc): A curved curtain or wall, usually white, used as a studio background to suggest unlimited space. Lights with colored gels can vary the look of the cyc.

Digital effects: Electronic creation of graphics and animated sequences using computer hardware and software designed specifically for the television industry.

Film chain: Projection equipment and video camera configured to transfer motion picture footage or 35mm slides to video tape.

Freeze frame: Technique of taking a single frame from a shot and "freezing" the action to create a still picture on video tape.

Interactive video: Programming that requires the viewer to take an active role in the presentation by performing tasks or making choices about the outcome of the material. When produced on video disc and combined with the random access features of computer-controlled playback equipment, programming can be designed to incorporate a large number of alternative nonlinear paths or routes through the material, a process known as branching.

M.O.S.: Abbreviation for footage shot without audio. Tradition has it the term comes from the early motion picture days when a German director working in America would call for shots "mit-out sound!" The mixed language version stuck.

P.O.V: Abbreviation for "point of view," used to indicate that the camera is positioned to represent the viewpoint of a character or individual in the program. The technique is also used to create a sense of viewer involvement when screen action is shot as though the viewer is on the scene seeing what the camera sees.

Presentational style: Dramatic writing in which the writer intentionally shatters the illusion of reality through dialog in which actors "break character" to address the audience or through striking use of stylized scenery, costumes or music.

Random access: The capability to access any frame of program material in a matter of seconds through the use of computer-controlled playback equipment.

Segue: (Pronounced seg-way.) Originally a smooth transition between musical numbers, generally involving an overlap or cross-fade. Today, the term is used more generally to describe transitions which involve overlapping audio and visual cues.

Super: Term used to indicate the superimposition of material over another picture. Most often used to indicate titles or text that is superimposed over another video image. (See Chapter 7.)

Time code: Refers to the signal encoded on video tape to provide a readout of elapsed time on the reel expressed in minutes, seconds and frame numbers. The Society of Motion Picture and Television Engineers, (SMPTE) has set a standard for recording the signal on video tape. Time codes are useful to the writer when selecting content from production footage to incorporate into a script. (See Chapter 9.)

Transitional effects: Television production terms used to describe the way in which one scene is joined to another. Writers frequently use the following terms to describe a transitional effect in the shooting script:

> FADE UP/FADE TO BLACK—All television programs begin and end in black. The very first image FADES UP from a black screen. The final images FADE TO BLACK. A momentary FADE TO BLACK can be used as a transition between major program segments.
> CUT—An instantaneous change between two shots.
> DISSOLVE—A momentary overlapping of two scenes. The tail end of Scene 1 fades out as the first frames of Scene 2 fade up. The two images overlap for a moment, creating a fluid transition which signals shifts in locale, time or content.
> WIPE—A visual effect as though Scene 1 is being wiped off the screen by the appearance of Scene 2. Wipes can take a variety of formats: horizontal, vertical, diagonal, etc. (See Chapter 6.)

Bibliography

BOOKS OF SPECIAL INTEREST

Floyd, Steve and Beth, ed., *Handbook of Interactive Video*. White Plains, NY: Knowledge Industry Publications, Inc., 1982.
   A practical guide to the field of interactive video with major sections on designing and writing interactive programming, defined as "any video program is which the sequence and selection of messages is determined by the user's response to the material."

Matrazzo, Donna, *The Corporate Scriptwriting Book*. Philadelphia, PA: Media Concepts Press, 1980.
   A practical guide on writing scripts for organizational communicators. Contains a wealth of useful forms and formats as models.

Rico, Gabriele Lusser, *Writing the Natural Way*. Los Angeles, CA: J.P. Tarcher, Inc., 1983.
   This nontraditional approach is intended to make writing more spontaneous by releasing the creative potential in the right hemisphere of the brain. Useful for developing a "pre-vision" and conceptual work leading to the television treatment.

Strunk, William, Jr. and E.B. White, *The Elements of Style*, third edition. New York, NY: Macmillan Publishing Co., Inc., 1979.
   A model of brevity and general English usage for any type of writing. Particularly appropos for writing direct, crisp narration.

OTHER USEFUL READINGS

Blum, Richard A., *Television Writing*. New York, NY: Hastings House Publishers, Inc., 1980.

Brady, John, *The Craft of the Screenwriter*. New York, NY: Simon and Schuster, 1981.

Brenner, Alfred, *The TV Scriptwriter's Handbook*. Cincinnati, OH: Writer's Digest Books, 1980.

Bronfeld, Stewart, *Writing for Film and Television*. Englewood Cliffs, NJ: Prentice-Hall, Inc., 1981.

Burr, Keith and Joseph Gillis, *The Screenwriter's Guide*. New York, NY: Zoetrope, Inc., 1982.

Coe, Michelle E., *How to Write for Television*. New York, NY: Crown Publishers, Inc., 1980.

Hall, Mark W., *Broadcast Journalism—An Introduction to News Writing*. New York, NY: Hastings House Publishers, Inc., 1978.

Hilliard, Robert L., *Writing for Television and Radio*. New York, NY: Hastings House Publishers, Inc., 1976.

Mager, Robert, *Preparing Instructional Objectives*, second edition. Belmont, CA: Pitman Learning, Inc., 1975.

Mager, Robert and Peter Pipe, *Analyzing Performance Problems, or You Really Oughta Wanna*. Belmont, CA: Pitman Learning, Inc., 1970.

Miller, William, *Screenwriting for Narrative Film and Television*. New York, NY: Hastings House Publishers, Inc., 1980.

Millerson, Gerald, *The Technique of Television Production*, tenth revised edition. New York, NY: Hastings House Publishers, Inc., 1979.

Rilla, Wolf, *The Writer and the Screen: On Writing for Film and Television*. New York, NY: William Morrow and Co., Inc., 1974.

Stempl, Tom, *Screenwriting*. San Diego, CA: A.S. Barnes and Co., 1982.

Straczynski, J. Michael, *The Complete Book of Scriptwrting*. Cincinnati, OH: Writer's Digest Books, 1982.

Swain, Dwight V., *Film Scriptwriting*. New York, NY: Hastings House Publishers, Inc., 1976.

Wylie, Max, *Writing for Television*. New York, NY: Cowles Book Co., Inc., 1970.

Zettl, Herbert, *Television Production Handbook*, third edition. Belmont, CA: Wadsworth, Inc., 1976.

Index

Action plan, 33, 55-56
Aspect ratio, 12, 51
Audience research, 2-4, 19, 22, 30, 34-38, 105, 202, 210
Audio transitions, 75-77

Behavioral objectives, 40-41
Branching in interactive video, 191-193

Camera directions, 65
Characterization, 144, 145-146, 152
Computer-aided instruction (CAI), 188
Conflict in dramatizations, 144, 147, 153
Content outline, 43-45, 127
Core question, 20
Custom transitional device, 73-75
Cut, 72

Dialog to convey content, 163-179
Dissolve, 72
Documentary style program, 120-121
Dramatizations in nonbroadcast television, 53, 142-145
  function of dramatic scenes, 147
  dramatic style, 153-162

Fade to black/fade up, 71-72
Flowcharts, 196, 202-203
Formats. See Page formats, Program formats
Freelance writers, 6, 8, 30, 109, 204-205, 213-215

Informational objectives, 39-40
Interview format, 52-53, 119-120, 122, 132-133

Interview sheets, 127, 130
Interactive video, 16, 17, 41, 202

Mixed formats, 53-54
Motion picture format, 77
Motivational objectives, 41-43

Narration, 103-109, 137-138
  narrative types, 101-102
Narrator
  character voice, 142
  off-camera, 101-102
  on-camera, 101
  nonprofessional, 102, 109, 116
Nonbroadcast networks, 15, 184
Nonbroadcast television market, 1-2
Nonlinear scripting, 195-196

Objectives, 23-24, 31-32, 38-43, 207, 211-212. See also Behavioral objectives, Informational objectives, Motivational objectives

Pacing, 67
Page formats, 67, 77, 80, 105-109, 116-118. See also Motion picture format, Split-page format, Storyboard.
Presentational style in dramas, 153
Program formats, 48-54. See also Interview format, Mixed formats, Talking head, Visuals and voices.
Programmed instruction, 183, 184-185, 188

Realistic style in dramas, 153
Research agenda, 22-31, 122, 124, 181, 207

Resolution. *See* Television screen resolution
Rough cut, 138-139

Script defined, 6
Scriptwriting process, 6-7
SMPTE time code, 134
Special effects transitions, 73
Special video effects, 99
Split-page format, 67-70, 105-109, 116-118
Storyboards, 80
Supers and titles, 97

Talking head, 49-50
  with props, 50-51
Television as a medium, 10-12, 14. *See also* Aspect ratio
Television screen resolution, 12-14, 51
Television continuum, 65

Television time, 51
Treatments, 47-48, 54-55, 126-127
  sample treatments, 58-64
Transitions. *See* Audio transitions, Video transitions.

Video cassettes, 15
Video column descriptions, 91-99
Video discs, 17, 183, 188-189
  writing for, 199-203
Video playback systems, 14-17
Video tape, 14
Video transitions, 71-75, 98-99. *See also* Custom transitional device, Cut, Dissolve, Fade to black/ fade up, Special effects transitions, Wipe
Visualization, 85-91, 210
Visuals and voices, 51-52

Wipe, 72

About the Author

William Van Nostran is a consultant in instructional design and scriptwriting services to corporate and institutional clients in the New York City area. He specializes in developing custom training and communications programs for private video cassette television networks. He has been an innovator in the use of video dramatizations for supervisory and management training. He has also taught on the college level and conducts seminars in video research and writing for Video Expo.

Before founding his consulting business, Van Nostran Associates, Mr. Van Nostran developed video programming for Owens-Corning Fiberglas Corporation and Crum & Forster Insurance Companies where he launched video cassette networks to support top management communications activities. He also served as a public information officer in the United States Air Force. Mr. Van Nostran is a graduate of the University of Wisconsin with a major in theater.

Other Titles Available from
Knowledge Industry Publications, Inc.

The Handbook of Interactive Video
edited by Steve and Beth Floyd
ISBN 0-86729-019-6   hardcover $34.95

The Executive's Guide to TV and Radio Appearances
by Michael Bland
ISBN 0-914236-53-9   hardcover $14.95

Managing the Corporate Media Center
by Eugene Marlow
ISBN 0-914236-68-7   hardcover $24.95

The Video Age: Television Technology and Applications in the 1980s
ISBN 0-86729-033-1   hardcover $29.95

Creating Original Programming for Cable TV
edited by Wm. Drew Shaffer and Richard Wheelwright
ISBN 0-86729-043-9   hardcover $29.95

Video Discs: The Technology, the Applications and the Future
by Efrem Sigel, Mark Schubin, Paul F. Merrill, et al.
ISBN 0-442-27784-9   softcover $16.95

Video in Health
edited by L. George Van Son
ISBN 0-914236-69-5   hardcover $29.95

Video in the Classroom: A Guide to Creative Television
by Don Kaplan
ISBN 0-914236-46-6   softcover $17.95

Available from Knowledge Industry Publications, Inc.
701 Westchester Ave.
White Plains, NY 10604